AT YOUR SIDE

Raymond Friel *and* David Wells

FOREWORD BY BILL HUEBSCH

AT

YOUR

SIDE

PRAYERS FOR
Messy, Delightful,
Complicated, Outrageous
EVERYDAY LIFE

TWENTY-THIRD
PUBLICATIONS

twentythirdpublications.com

TWENTY-THIRD PUBLICATIONS
One Montauk Avenue, Suite 200
New London, CT 06320
(860) 437-3012 or (800) 321-0411
www.twentythirdpublications.com

The Scripture quotations contained herein are from the *New Revised
Standard Version of the Bible*, copyrighted 1989 by the Division of Christian
Education of the National Council of the Churches of Christ in the United
States of America, and are used by permission. All rights reserved.

Cover image: VarnaK / Shutterstock.com
Interior layout designed by Emma Repetti

ISBN: 978-1-62785-600-3
Printed in Canada.

 A division of Bayard, Inc.

Dedications

In memory of my mother, Ellen Friel, who died on 4 May 2019: may she rest in eternal peace; and for my brother, Martin, who carries her grace.

Raymond Friel

For Margaret, mother and friend, who never got to read these prayers, but inspired them by her devotion to a life of prayer.

David Wells

"These heartfelt prayers will surely help all those pilgrims of the inner life who are looking to experience the divine source through surrender and vulnerability – and then to face into the everyday with renewed courage and generosity. The honesty of these prayers will surely help you encounter the heart of God."

Fr. Richard Rohr OFM, author and international speaker

"In these wonderful, fresh and hope-filled prayers, our everyday worries and anxieties are embraced by the eternal Word of God. Nothing is too ordinary or pedestrian to be unworthy of being brought to God's kind presence. Here we are indeed offered daily bread to sustain us on the journey."

Fr. Timothy Radcliffe OP, author and international speaker

"This is a prayer book for real people who are looking for a guide to help them speak with Jesus. It's the book for which I've been searching over the past five years. The prayers are honest and written in the language of everyday life. I'd like to put this into the hands of everyone who wants to 'show up for prayer' and have a bit of help to get rolling. Wonderful."

Bill Huebsch, author of many books, including *Promise and Hope: Pastoral Theology in the Age of Mercy* (Twenty-Third Publications and Novalis, 2020)

"So many of us struggle to believe that God loves each of us personally, and so is interested in all aspects of our daily lives; we often find personal prayer difficult.

In *At Your Side,* the authors of this beautiful, insightful, and sometimes challenging collection of prayers wish to help us to see that prayer is a heart-to-heart encounter with God, who loves us passionately, desires that we share our daily lives with him, and who wants us to know that there is nothing that we experience that we cannot share with him in prayer. Raymond Friel and David Wells, who have so much experience of working with parishioners, teachers, chaplains and catechists, reveal through these prayers that our very lives can be a prayer, indeed an adventure, as we allow God to be at our side and so help us to walk in his ways.

At Your Side is indeed a most instructive and encouraging book for anyone to dip into, especially those who pray, those who want to pray, and those who are called upon to lead others in prayer. I warmly commend it to you!"

+Patrick McKinney, Bishop of Nottingham

"This beautiful collection of prayers gives us just the right words to soothe and uplift the soul in every situation and helps us to find God in each moment of our daily life.

This is a book of prayers to use again and again. A treasured companion for the days, months and years ahead."

Dame Rachel de Souza, CEO of Inspiration Trust

"*At Your Side* is one of the most helpful, creative and easily accessible prayer materials available today. It is an essential resource for all who are seeking to deepen their own prayer life and bring others into ways of praying that are refreshing and relevant in the world of today."

Sr. Judith Russi SSMN, author and Director of EducareM

Contents

Foreword

A few years ago, I was part of a fantastic parish softball team. We won almost all our games, which seemed miraculous to me, a non-athlete. I was really hoping we might win the final tournament because I'd never won a single athletic trophy in my life, and this seemed to be my moment.

On the morning of the final game, I decided to go down to the parish church and ask God for victory. I wasn't precisely sure God behaved in this way. I wasn't sure God intervened directly in parish softball games, but I really wanted to win, and I thought I'd hedge my bets and cover all my bases, as it were. Anyway, what could it hurt?

So, I headed off to pray. But as I pushed open the door of the small church, I was horrified to find that the entire opposing team was already there! They beat me to it! They had asked first, and besides, I was outnumbered! They were all there. I could see there was no hope!

For many people, prayer is a sort of consumer commodity. We pray for things: rain, peace, health, success – or victory in the big game. And when we get what we ask for, we believe our prayer is responsible for it. If we don't get it, we switch into another way of thinking and wonder whether we prayed wrong, or whether God just knew better, or whether someone else deserved to win this one more than we did. Or maybe we were just outnumbered: more people were praying for the opposite result, forcing God to go with the majority.

We think of prayer as something we do to receive something else. It's a commodity to be traded for favours from God, who, in our judgment, would not bestow these favours without sufficient supplication.

This simplified view of prayer is in tension with what we learn in Scripture. When we listen to the Gospels, we see that prayer is indeed "receiving," but what is received is the energy and love of God in the life of the one who prays. Prayer orients us towards God, who is the Force of Life, the Creator, the Artist in the garden, who made us all.

Our role in prayer is simply to pause and allow prayer to emerge in us naturally. It is for us to turn down the volume of our own words long enough to hear the word of God. It is for us to listen. To listen. God is speaking if we would only listen.

As I first read the prayers in this book, I found myself putting the book down in my lap to pause. My heart lingered with the prayers, moving me towards God, resting in God's love. These prayers didn't end at the "Amen" but, instead, launched me into contemplation and reflection. This is a prayer book I want to keep near me.

Let me take you back with me to that small parish church on the morning of the big game. I did finally go in that morning, still intending to ask God for victory. I knelt down, realizing I was in the heart of the enemy.

The coach of the other team was leading a prayer. But he wasn't praying for victory! He was praying for charity, for fairness, and for an honest game. He asked God for the inner strength to be a humble winner – or a graceful loser – and he prayed that, in the final analysis, our lives together in our parish would be made more joyful, that our community would grow stronger from this contest on the playing field.

Well, for Pete's sake, I thought. I knew he was right. His prayer wasn't a bargain with God but an opening of his heart to goodness and fair play. I learned something that day that I've never forgotten. It's something I've heard Pope Francis promise us as well. If we take a step towards Jesus, he will not disappoint us. Jesus walks with us and accompanies us every day. Prayer opens our hearts to that and leads us to accompany one another as well. So, in the end, God is indeed "at our side," as this prayer book helps us understand, but we are also at one another's side as companions on the journey, as accompanists in faith. And here's a big Amen to that!

Bill Huebsch

Introduction
Why we wrote *At Your Side*

In Luke's Gospel the disciples say to Jesus, "Teach us to pray." This request is made because they see in Jesus something they hope for. Jesus can live the things he teaches. Jesus is not paralyzed by worry, he loves generously, he acts justly, he doesn't court popularity and he doesn't engineer advantage for himself. The disciples see in Jesus who they want to become. To realize their hope, the followers know they must connect to a divine strength. In reply, Jesus offers them what must have first seemed like dangerous words: the Lord's Prayer. The prayer would have felt radical in many ways. It is shockingly familiar in its assertion that we, too, may call God "Our Father." It also entwines God's actions with our own, "as we forgive." God's activity in the heavenly realm is to become ours in the earthly realm.

The prayer Jesus gave us is a gift to all Christians. It encompasses all we need to say. Yet, in learning and repeating it we can begin to lose the very intimacy and action the prayer itself compels. It is possible to say these words and yet remain a stone's throw from the Father. The language of our inherited prayers is essential to a life of faith and community, but it points us in the direction of yet another language, a language more intimate still, a humble and childlike language.

In frequent appeals, Pope Francis draws our attention to the importance of a personal encounter with the divine. This encounter is often personal, deeply honest and eventually wordless. To achieve it we need a sense of God's presence. This presence is not "beginners'" Christianity. It is what we are about as Christians; without it, we will find ourselves living by willpower rather than God power. Pope Francis puts it like this:

1

"Jesus Christ loves you; he gave his life to save you; and now he is living at your side every day to enlighten, strengthen and free you." This first proclamation is called "first" not because it exists at the beginning and can then be forgotten or replaced by other more important things. It is first in a qualitative sense, because it is the principal proclamation, the one which we must hear again and again in different ways.[1]

To have Jesus at "our side" is not only a question of faith, because it also demands imagination. It calls for us to involve Jesus in what first appear to be quite trivial matters. When we begin to do this, we grow in our conviction that the very things that delight us delight him, the very things that distress us distress him, and we grow in friendship. To those of us for whom prayer has been a formal experience, this type of encounter can be troubling: "Can Jesus really be that entwined in the personal circumstances and situations of my daily life?" We are called to persevere. As we begin to talk to Jesus in this way, our conversation becomes a relationship. It is then that we begin to enjoy the accompaniment of Jesus, as he once accompanied the disciples at Emmaus. As Pope Francis suggests: "To be friends with God means to pray with simplicity, like children talking to their parents."[2]

This book does not draw attention away from the inherited prayers of our traditions. Far from it. This book encourages you to begin to see the ordinary and everyday circumstances of your lives as an opportunity to fulfill those inherited prayers. When you delight, learn to cast your eyes to heaven in utter gratitude. When you are distressed, learn to stretch out an empty hand as a beggar before God. These things happen as a result of the things life throws at us. So here is a collection of prayers drawn from the messy, delightful, complicated, outrageous and mundane things of life. As you read them, allow them to encourage your own inner dialogue. Notice that in the most unexpected circumstances, Jesus will begin to accompany you. He will accompany you out of the confines of time set aside for prayer and into the Monday mornings. Sometimes God is going to speak to you through the difficult meeting at work, the woman at the bus stop, or the pregnancy test. It's not all walking on water!

The aim of this book is to encourage all Christians to build upon the many great written prayers of our tradition, so that with fresh eyes we will encounter Jesus at our side, every day, to enlighten, strengthen and free us. Once that begins to happen, your life will become a prayer and every day an opportunity for adventure. In the end, your prayer will become all about what God is doing, and you may return to those inherited words in a much more intimate way: "Thy will be done."

Don't read this book cover to cover. Consult the titles in the contents or just dip into it. May you encounter Jesus in the reading and discover that you and the world around you are the work of the Father, brought to life by the Spirit. May prayer help you to enjoy your life.

Raymond Friel and David Wells
October 2019

Morning Prayer (I)

Lord, help me to be still for a few moments
   before the day begins,
to be still and know that you are God,
the God who made me and knows me and loves me.

Help me to be silent
   and in the silence to trust in the presence
   of your Spirit within me –
my rock, my shield, my deepest me.

When you are praying, do not heap up empty phrases
as the Gentiles do; for they think that they will be heard
because of their many words. Do not be like them, for
your Father knows what you need before you ask him.

Matthew 6:7-8

Morning Prayer (II)

Lord, thank you for this new day –
another chance to become my better self,
to learn from yesterday, to go again,
to open up to your Spirit, prompting me to what gives life.
Help me to recognize in my moods,
in my annoyance at the moments that could have gone better,
in the glimpses of love for loved ones,
your Spirit within me, your voice in the sanctuary of my soul –
my true self, my conscience –
and help me to act on those promptings, trusting that this is you
    shaping me, moulding me with infinite patience
    and love, like a parent
    with a wayward,
    wilful child.

Yet, O LORD, you are our Father;
we are the clay, and you are our potter;
we are all the work of your hand.

Isaiah 64:8

There is no bad way to pray and there is no starting point for
prayer. All the great spiritual masters offer only one non-
negotiable rule: you have to show up for prayer and you
have to show up regularly. Everything else is negotiable and
respects your unique circumstances.

Ronald Rolheiser, Prayer: Our Deepest Longing[3]

◆ Morning Prayer (III)

Lord, give me a big heart today,
a generosity of spirit in all my encounters,
especially the interruptions, the moments of grace
   by the side of the road, the chance to step in and help.
Give me the grace to be really present in the presence of others,
to see the "sacred grandeur" of my neighbour,
to listen well, to take the first step towards them,
to let go of my well-earned assumptions;
to give less offence,
to take offence less easily.
Give me the grace to see the needs of the world around me,
to see through normality,
to see injustice hidden in plain sight.
Give me the grace to see in the most ordinary moments of encounter
   the graced reality of our world.

> May I have the courage today
> To live the life that I would love,
> To postpone my dream no longer,
> But do at last what I came here for
> And waste my heart on fear no more.
>
> John O'Donohue, *Benedictus: A Book of Blessings*[4]

Morning Prayer (IV)

Lord, I pray for those who need my prayers today,
who need my attention, my best thinking,
   my most generous gesture.
Help me to see where I might bring blessing and consolation.
I pray for those I love, that I may love them better.
I pray for those I do not love, or those I'm indifferent toward:
that I will be moved to see them in a new light,
to see the world from their point of view,
to see the seed of your presence in them.

I pray for those for whom this day is not welcome,
those for whom life is a struggle.
Teach me how to see, judge and act as I should,
to build up the kingdom of love
   and resist the kingdom of violence.

Thank you, Lord, for this day,
for the gift of this life,
the new creation.

> Let me hear of your steadfast love in the morning,
> for in you I put my trust.
> Teach me the way I should go,
> for to you I lift up my soul.
>
> Psalm 143:8

> The aim of prayer, in fact, is to attain that point where we
> do the will of God, not that God should do our will. Our
> prayers do not change the plan of God's love for us, but it
> is the gifts which God grants in prayer which transform
> us and which bring us into harmony with his will.
>
> Enzo Bianchi, *Why Pray, How to Pray*[5]

Morning Prayer (V)

Father,
creator God,
source of life and love,
God for us,
be the solid ground I walk on today.

Son,
God in our skin,
Revelation of the Father,
God with us,
be the friend who walks beside me today.

Spirit,
spark of resurrection,
drop in the pool of conscience,
God in us,
be the goodness in my heart today.

Glory be to the Father,
and to the Son and to the Holy Spirit.
As it was in the beginning, is now
    and ever shall be.
World without end.

Amen.

> There is only one God... The Father, the Son, and the Holy Spirit
> is each God... The Father, the Son, and the Holy Spirit are not the
> same... Our flawed and fragile thoughts and words are not up to
> the job of giving a full, wholly sufficient description of the Most
> High. It is God who is the Truth, the whole Truth, and nothing
> but the Truth... and *not* our witness statements about him.
>
> Stephen Bullivant, *The Trinity: How Not to Be a Heretic*[6]

Morning prayer at the end of the week

Lord, as we come to the end of the week,
help me to see when I was closest to you,
when I felt your presence,
when you had a message for me,
when I felt consolation.
And help me to see when I was distant from you,
when the thinking I indulged in,
my actions or lack of action, prevented me from hearing
what you were saying to me, when I felt desolation.
Help me to cope with my tiredness today,
so that I don't say or do anything
    that is not me, not my better self, the self you want me to be.

I look forward to the weekend, a time for rest,
a time to spend with those I love, or try to love,
a time to restore the balance, visit the wells, wander the hills.
But help me not to see my downtime as just about my needs;
catch me when I'm shaping the world around my pleasures,
give me a heart for the vulnerable of the world
    and a desire to spend some of my time, my free time,
helping where I can.

We live in a world that is for the most part spiritually tone-deaf, where all the goods are in the store window, digitized, or reduced to a flat screen. And so, prayer is a struggle. So are a lot of other things. When the surface is all there is, it is hard to be enchanted by anything, to see depth, to be deeply touched by poetry, faith and love.

Ronald Rolheiser, *Prayer: Our Deepest Longing* [7]

Meanwhile, the Gospel tells us constantly to run the risk of a face-to-face encounter with others, with their physical presence which challenges us, with their pain and their pleas... True faith in the incarnate Son of God is inseparable from self-giving, from membership in the community, from service, from reconciliation with others. The Son of God, by becoming flesh, summoned us to the revolution of tenderness.

Pope Francis, *Evangelii Gaudium* ("The Joy of the Gospel")[8]

Personal reflection

- How do I start my day?

- Do I make any time to still myself, to encounter the divine, to pray?

- Do I take any time to try and recognize the presence of God in everyday events?

10

◆ When I feel sorrow for another – See it. Say it. Sort it out[9]

To the young mom soaked to the skin,
  pushing her stroller up a hill:
  send your Spirit, Lord.
To the woman in the supermarket
  patiently waiting for the bread to be reduced in price:
  send your Spirit, Lord.
To the man who's placing a bet, just one more time:
  send your Spirit, Lord.
To parents waving goodbye to grown-up children as they leave home:
  send your Spirit, Lord.
To seniors whose cherished garden is becoming a source of stress:
  send your Spirit, Lord.
To the driver now living with regret that he wasn't watching
  when he pulled out:
  send your Spirit, Lord.
To the job applicant making the long journey home wishing she
  hadn't applied:
  send your Spirit, Lord.
To the thief in the train station who needed the laptop
  to feed an addiction:
  send your Spirit, Lord.
To the person in the waiting room waiting for a diagnosis:
  send your Spirit, Lord.
To the lonely man in the corner store who is taking forever
  to buy lottery tickets:
  send your Spirit, Lord.

To the timid child who fears going back to school every Sunday night:
send your Spirit, Lord.
To the victim struggling to escape the memory:
send your Spirit, Lord.

Loving Father, so many people struggle behind the veneer of a smile.
Open the eyes of my heart, Lord.
Help me to encounter people with a heart that sees.
May I see it, say it and, if possible, sort it out.
Everywhere.

Amen.

> The Christian's programme – the programme of the Good
> Samaritan, the programme of Jesus – is "a heart which sees."
> This heart sees where love is needed and acts accordingly.
> Pope Benedict XVI, *Deus Caritas Est* ("God is Love")[10]

Personal reflection

- When does your heart recognize the plight of other
  people, drawing you in to an experience of compassion?

When I need to lighten up a bit

Lord, come off the pages of my Bible and into my life. Come out of the Order of Service and the beautifully crafted prayer books and into my Mondays and Fridays. Fall out of the canvas and off every Renaissance painting. Leap out of the art galleries:

that your joy may be in me and my joy complete.

Lord, push aside the clutter and jumble and the piles of paperwork. Break into a house full of things I bought, and things I have acquired and things I don't use. Cast out these distractions I have accumulated:

that your joy may be in me and my joy complete.

Lord, disturb my business as usual. Derail my regular commute. Fill in the rut I have dug for myself. Open my mind to the possibility of conversion. Break through the concrete blocks of my set ways and established routines:

that your joy may be in me and my joy complete.

Lord, pierce the armour of sought solitude, my all-inclusive deal to avoid other people. Open my heart to the traffic around me. Prevent me from building bigger walls, growing higher hedges and buying stronger padlocks:

that your joy may be in me and my joy complete.

Lord, prise open my silent lips and my mouth shall declare your praise. Breathe new harmony into my song. Grant fresh strength to these tired limbs. Help me to dance when you play the tune. Help me to proclaim from the rooftops when you send the words:

that your joy may be in me and my joy complete.

Lord, open my tear ducts. Raise my gaze to the needs of others. Alert my eyes to a bigger world. Come into the upper room of my heart and break open the doors of self-infatuation. Propel me beyond myself:

that your joy may be in me and my joy complete.

Lord, crease the smooth skin of my face into laugh lines. Reveal to me the joy of Mary's "Let it be done to me" which awoke in her the Magnificat. May your joy spill out of me like it did from the shepherds at your birth, from St. Philip Neri, St. Thomas More and St. Vincent de Paul:[11]

that your joy may be in me and my joy complete.

> I have said these things to you so that my joy may be in you, and that your joy may be complete.
>
> John 15:11

Personal reflection

- What does it mean to be joyful?

Prayer for a community at the beginning of the week

God our Father,
at the beginning of another week,
help us to remember why we are here
   and not to be tempted away from our mission
   by what is expedient.
Help us to remember especially our mission to those
   who are vulnerable and marginal,
those who most need our help.

As we look ahead to another week,
we pray for the intentions of the community –
for the grace to meet the particular challenges we face,
for the generosity to remember the needs of others,
to make room for each other.
Let us never become so busy that we overlook
   the human need in front of us;
that we look after the brother or sister in our midst
   who is struggling, who needs to be carried for a while.

Help us to be wise
   in our use of authority,
to be civil and respectful in all our encounters.
And when disagreements arise
   may we use patient dialogue, empathy and imagination
   to resolve our differences.

We commend our work to you –
keep us humble, keep us mindful,
that any good that comes of what we do
   is your work in the world, not ours.
We plant the seeds that one day will grow.
We are the workers, not the master builder.

St. [patron], pray for us.
Our Lady of Perpetual Help, pray for us.

We make all our prayers through Christ our Lord.
Amen.

> As God's chosen ones, holy and beloved, clothe yourselves with compassion, kindness, humility, meekness, and patience. Bear with one another and, if anyone has a complaint against another, forgive each other; just as the Lord has forgiven you, so you also must forgive.
>
> Colossians 3:12-13

> A spirituality of communion indicates above all the heart's contemplation of the mystery of the Trinity dwelling in us, and whose light we must also be able to see shining on the face of the brothers and sisters around us.
>
> St. John Paul II, Novo Millennio Ineunte
("At the Beginning of the New Millennium")[12]

A future not our own

We accomplish in our lifetime
only a tiny fraction
of the magnificent enterprise
that is God's work.
Nothing we do is complete,
which is another way of saying
that the Kingdom always lies beyond us.

No statement says all that could be said.
No prayer fully expresses our faith.
No confession brings perfection.
No pastoral visit brings wholeness.
No programme accomplishes
    the Church's mission.
No set of goals and objectives
    includes everything.

Attributed to St. Oscar Romero[13]

◆ In the middle of the day

Lord, I need a moment,
I need a time out
to remember
your presence deep within me,
within the good earth,
within my very desire to take a moment.
Help me to be silent and still,
to settle again into the now,
the only place I will ever find you.
Help me to keep the business of the day
in some kind of perspective;
to remember that, whatever happens,
this too will pass.

Help me with the anxieties
that are always there, like a headache –
the loved ones I worry about,
the work pressures that sometimes overwhelm me,
the colleagues I don't get along with.
Help me to be loving and thoughtful,
to listen when I need to,
to be present to those in front of me,
to be brave when I need to be brave
and to sense your presence in all my encounters.

> For I am convinced that neither death, nor life, nor angels, nor
> rulers, nor things present, nor things to come, nor powers, nor
> height, nor depth, nor anything else in all creation, will be able
> to separate us from the love of God in Christ Jesus our Lord.
>
> Romans 8:38-39

When I'm wasting time

Deadlines met, mission accomplished, adrenaline over and now I'm stuck in a tired café on the subway platform. Of all places. I'm still rushing, yet I'm not moving. What I could be doing with this empty pause? What stopped me in my tracks on this platform? My time wasted by things beyond my control.

Open my eyes, Lord. Help me to see your face.
Open my eyes, Lord. Help me to see.

The tiled floor in front of me is dimpled into a thousand peaks and crevices, and between them sits a tiny drop of rainwater. The blackened floor glistens. The sun finds its way through a heavy sky. The empty potato chip bag underneath my seat swirls in a sudden breeze. Be annoyed or pick it up?

Open my eyes, Lord. Help me to see your face.
Open my eyes, Lord. Help me to see.

Another thud from the vending machine behind me. Put your money in and the spiral unwinds. Sugar and salt to distract and delight. All that choice just waiting to fall. I'll put this empty chip bag of mine into the garbage can and drop a full bag out of that machine.

Open my eyes, Lord. Help me to see your face.
Open my eyes, Lord. Help me to see.

Now I'm bored. Pull out the phone. Look at it. Who's there? Someone to talk to, someone to text, some unfinished business, surely? There must be a conversation to tear me away from all this delay. I'll get busy, that's what I'll do: an email or two.

Open my eyes, Lord. Help me to see your face.
Open my eyes, Lord. Help me to see.

"Excuse me," she says. "Is that seat taken?" Of course it isn't... how did my bag find its way there? "No, not at all," I say, removing my accessories. She is calm. She rummages around a bottomless bag, pulling out headphones, a cereal bar and a thick book about politics. She is soon far away in her own world.

Open my eyes, Lord. Help me to see your face.
Open my eyes, Lord. Help me to see.

This stranger sits next to me. I know nothing of her anxiety, her aspiration, her joy, but it is all here sitting serenely next to me for this short moment in eternity. Lord, whoever this woman is, I thank you for her. You know her name. Whoever she hopes to become, whatever she hopes to achieve, wherever this journey may take her, I pray for her now. Complete in her the work you began when you created her, and help me to find an opportunity like this in every unplanned pause.

Open my eyes, Lord. Help me to see your face.
Open my eyes, Lord. Help me to see.

They came to Bethsaida. Some people brought a blind man to him and begged him to touch him. He took the blind man by the hand and led him out of the village; and when he had put saliva on his eyes and laid his hands on him, he asked him, "Can you see anything?" And the man looked up and said, "I can see people, but they look like trees, walking." Then Jesus laid his hands on his eyes again; and he looked intently and his sight was restored, and he saw everything clearly.

Mark 8:22-25

Personal reflection

- When do I recognize my own blindness and how do my eyes open to God's way of seeing?

A prayer at the end of the day

Lord, as the day comes to an end
help me to settle for a moment in your presence…
to be still and set aside the agitations of the day,
to be grateful for my life,
for the gift of everything.

Help me now to consider the day –
to let the events play out,
my encounters with people, my thoughts,
my reactions to unexpected moments, to interruptions.
What rises in me when I think of today?
What plays on my mind? What tugs at my heart?
What drained me of life?
What enlivened me?
What stretched me a little into being?
What diminished me?

What did I do for others
that was helpful, that was unhelpful?
Did I say anything to demean another,
to get one over, one up?
Where might I have been more attentive?
What in my lifestyle remains unexamined
that I know is unhealthy, selfish, unsustainable?
What am I sorry for?
Where did I fall again?

What is going to change?

Where does your Spirit need to get at me,

to make me more forgiving, more compassionate, more patient,

more committed to my neighbour?

Lord, bless all those I love this night.

Keep us from fear and anxiety

and bring us safely to a new day, with new purpose

and a new desire to change, to grow,

to be our better selves.

> When someone experiences laughter or tears, bears responsibility, stands by the truth, breaks through the egoism in his life with other people; when someone hopes against hope, faces the shallowness and stupidity of the daily rush and bustle with humour and patience, refusing to be embittered; when someone learns to be silent and in this inner silence lets the evil in his heart die rather than spread outward; in a word, whenever someone lives as he would like to live, combating his own egoism and the continual temptation to inner despair – there is an event of grace.
>
> Karl Rahner, "Secular Life and the Sacraments"[14]

When I can't pray[15]

Lord, I can't pray. I don't know how to pray.
I don't even know if I want to pray.
The well has run dry.
I'm so busy these days, how can I find time for prayer?
I don't even know what to say anymore.
When I was a child, we said our prayers. It seemed so simple,
but now I wonder, *what's the point?*
If we're all praying for different things, why do some prayers
    get answered and some don't?
And why is it that good people who pray still suffer
    and others, who don't, seem to flourish?
Prayer feels like I'm talking to myself in an empty room.

My child, so many questions,
so much anxiety in your heart.
Do not be afraid, do not worry, I am with you,
whether you know that or not,
whether you feel it or not.
I know you struggle with prayer,
I know that you don't know how to pray
    but you don't have to: my Spirit will pray in you.
All you need to do is bring your troubled heart to the well.
There I will meet you.
Let go of your fears; extend your hand to me.
That is all I want, more than anything: an open hand and heart,
a humble heart.
There I will find a home.

Likewise the Spirit helps us in our weakness; for we do not know how to pray as we ought, but that very Spirit intercedes with sighs too deep for words. And God, who searches the heart, knows what is the mind of the Spirit, because the Spirit intercedes for the saints according to the will of God.

Romans 8:26-27

Jesus said to her, "Everyone who drinks of this water will be thirsty again, but those who drink of the water that I will give them will never be thirsty. The water that I will give will become in them a spring of water gushing up to eternal life."

John 4:13-14

The wonder of prayer is revealed beside the well where we come seeking water: there, Christ comes to meet every human being. It is he who first seeks us and asks us for a drink. Jesus thirsts; his asking arises from the depths of God's desire for us. Whether we realise it or not, prayer is the encounter of God's thirst with ours. God thirsts that we may thirst for him.

Catechism of the Catholic Church, 2560

Softness, and peace, and joy, and love, and bliss,
Exalted manna, gladness of the best,
Heaven in ordinary, man well drest,
The milky way, the bird of Paradise,
Church-bells beyond the stars heard, the soul's blood,
The land of spices; something understood.

From "Prayer," by George Herbert[16]

◆ When I'm losing my religion

A thief came in the night. I wasn't looking. I didn't notice at first. Everything in the house seemed just as it always was. The valuables sat in their usual boxes, the keys still hanging on their hooks. All in the house was tidy: linen folded, shirts ironed, food in the pantry. There was no sign of disturbance, no smashed windows or broken locks. In the absence of any obvious damage I carried on as normal, finishing the list of things to do and going about my business as usual. Ahh, business as usual. Leaving and returning day by day, week by week, month by month. It was a fine routine. Everything was just as it should be. Why wouldn't it be? Nothing was disturbed. But it wasn't the house the thief broke into.

I woke up this morning to discover my enthusiasm had gone. All I could find in that space was cynicism. I woke up to discover that my humour had gone. All I could find in that space was self-importance. I woke up this morning to discover that patience was no longer in the hallway. All I could find there was anxiety. It was as though I had been in a fight, but there were no bruises. The thief came in the night while I wasn't looking and all the locks and security lights didn't alert me.

Lord, I was going to make a difference. I was going to enjoy the adventure. I was going to be compassionate. I find myself in a tidy house called *business as usual*. Turns out the thief didn't steal my things, he stole me.

Lord, help me to keep watch, to be alert to the loss of the virtues you gave me, before it is too late.

Amen.

> The thief comes only to steal and kill and destroy. I came that they may have life, and have it abundantly.
>
> John 10:10

Personal reflection

- What virtues are you losing, or have you lost?

- Is it time to pray for the recovery of a lost virtue?

◆ When you don't know who to turn to

So, you have lost your dream, abandoned your plan, walked away from what you believed, your hope now evaporated. Look to Jesus. Jesus stands before you as once he stood before the dead son of the widow and with the power of his resurrection he urges you: "Young man, young woman, arise!"

So, darkness has descended. You are blinded and unable to find the light. Your life has shrink-wrapped around you. You can't find your way out. Turn to Jesus. Jesus stands before you as once he stood before Lazarus' tomb and with all the power of his resurrection he urges you: "Lazarus, come out."

So, life has wounded you. You do not know who to turn to. Who can you trust? You feel dead inside. Call to Jesus. Jesus reaches out as once he reached out to the little girl and with all the power of his resurrection he urges you: "Talitha cum!" which means, "little girl, get up!"

So, you feel worthless and guilty. You can't shake off your shame. You know you made a mistake but you can't find a way out. You hide from your own thoughts. Sit before Jesus. Jesus looks with love as once he did towards the woman with an alabaster jar and with all the power of his resurrection he assures you: "Your sins are forgiven."

So, you are powerless. You have lost confidence. You have learned to hide behind others. You have become invisible, dependent, a shadow of your former self. Call upon Jesus. Jesus greets you as once he greeted the man at Bethesda and with all the power of his resurrection he commands you: "Get up! Pick up your mat and walk."

Reign in me, Lord. That I may rise above the things that deaden, bind, poison, enslave and exhaust my spirit. By your strength, call me to arise, out of the tombs I find myself in, that I may live the life you offer.

Amen.

> If you have lost your inner vitality, your dreams, your enthusiasm, your optimism and your generosity, Jesus stands before you as once he stood before the dead son of the widow, and with all the power of his resurrection he urges you: "Young man, I say to you, arise!"
>
> Pope Francis, *Christus Vivit* ("Christ is Alive")[17]

Personal reflection

- What defeats you?

- Is it time to call upon God to raise you out of the tomb of your own making?

On the need to wake up

A prayer for Advent

Lord, at this time of year
the message of the world is *have what you want.*
Have what you never knew you wanted
   until you saw it on this glamorous one,
until you saw the neighbour's new smartphone,
their children in the latest running shoes.
The message of the world is *this is who you are.*
To be somebody means to be turned out
in the brands that signify success,
to watch movies in a home theatre,
to live in a quiet part of town with a driveway
   to park the new car.

Your word strikes a different note –
snap out of it, wake up from this dream of the world,
change the direction in which you're looking for happiness.
This life diminishes the soul.
You'll never have enough of what you think you want in this world,
just more and more of what you don't need.
Lord, there are times I'd rather keep it that way.
I like my *things*, my home comforts, the luxuries I "deserve."
I like a glass or two, from time to time.
What's so wrong with that? I work hard. I'm a burden to no one,
but still your voice, the voice of your prophet
   in the wilderness
   disturbs my comfort.

Lord, give me the grace to change,
to examine my life – what I do, what I desire –
and take the first steps on a new way, to be open
to the gift beneath the glitter.

Do not be afraid, little flock, for it is your Father's good pleasure to give you the kingdom. Sell your possessions, and give alms. Make purses for yourselves that do not wear out, an unfailing treasure in heaven, where no thief comes near and no moth destroys. For where your treasure is, there your heart will be also.

Luke 12:32-34

We have been the recipients of the choicest bounties of heaven. We have been preserved, these many years, in peace and prosperity. We have grown in numbers, wealth and power, as no other nation has ever grown. But we have forgotten God.

Abraham Lincoln[18]

Sabbath is the cessation of widely shared practices of acquisitiveness. It provides time, space, energy and imagination for coming to the ultimate recognition that more commodities, which may be acquired in the rough and ready of daily economics, finally do not satisfy. Sabbath is variously restraint, withdrawal, or divestment from the concrete practices of society that specialize in anxiety. Sabbath is an antidote to anxiety that both derives from our craving and in turn feeds those cravings for more. Sabbath is an arena in which to recognize that we live by gift and not by possession, that we are satisfied by relationships of attentive fidelity and not by amassing commodities. We know in the gospel tradition that we may indeed "gain the whole world" and lose our souls (Mark 8:34-37). Thus Sabbath is soul-receiving when we are in a posture of receptivity before our Father who knows we need them (Luke 12:30).

Walter Brueggemann, Sabbath as Resistance[19]

Hedonism and consumerism can prove our downfall, for when we are obsessed with our own pleasure, we end up being all too concerned about ourselves and our rights, and we feel a desperate need for free time to enjoy ourselves. We will find it hard to feel and show any real concern for those in need, unless we are able to cultivate a certain simplicity of life, resisting the feverish demands of a consumer society, which leave us impoverished and unsatisfied, anxious to have it all now.

Pope Francis, *Gaudete et Exsultate*[20]

Annunciation

Was the messenger
a young man, beautiful to behold,
or a feathered explosion of light –
a day of chores and grinding repetition shattered
by divine visitation?

Or was it more a sharp knowing
at the well that morning, drawing water
from a pool that clouded over,
the voices of the others fading
as the question of the ages formed in your heart?

Hail Mary,
most highly favoured one,
whose "yes" was the key to unlock the door of salvation,
God-bearer, mother of God, mother of the Church,
pray for us sinners: now,

in this valley of history,
in this flicker of time we've been given
to respond to the invitation as you did;
and at the hour of our death.

Amen.

Our soul waits for the Lord;
he is our help and shield.
Our heart is glad in him,
because we trust in his holy name.
Let your steadfast love, O LORD, be upon us,
even as we hope in you.

Psalm 33:20-22

Then the angel departed from her.

Luke 1:38

On the basis of the angel's "*Kecharitomene*", Mary has been called "full of grace" (*charis* is the Greek for "grace"), and this means, basically, that she is someone who is profoundly disposed to receive gifts. In this, she becomes the new Eve, the mother of all those who would be reborn by being receptive to God's life as a gift.

Robert Barron, *Catholicism*[21]

Into this world, this demented inn in which there is absolutely no room for him at all, Christ has come uninvited. But because He cannot be at home in it, because He is out of place in it, and yet He must be in it, His place is with those others for whom there is no room. His place is with those who do not belong, who are rejected by power because they are regarded as weak, those who are discredited, who are denied the status of persons, tortured, exterminated. With those for whom there is no room, Christ is present in this world.

Thomas Merton, *Raids on the Unspeakable*[22]

A prayer for life

Lord, we thank you for the gift of life –
our own life, the lives of our loved ones,
the lives of those we don't love,
the life that erupts around us every spring.

We pray for those who are fragile,
those whose lives are precarious
and depend on others –

for the unborn, helpless in the womb,
for the very old, in a twilight of waiting,
for the migrants, clinging to hope,
for the exploited, imprisoned in fear,
for the condemned, hurried to death at the hands of others.

We pray for those with influence
over the lives of their fellow human beings,
over those who are helpless –

for mothers who carry life within them,
for the caregivers and visitors,
for the border patrol,
for the entrepreneurs,
for those who sit in judgment,

help them to see
the beauty of the lives in their care,
to do no harm,
but work for its flourishing.

For surely I know the plans I have for you, says the LORD, plans for your welfare and not for harm, to give you a future with hope.

Jeremiah 29:11

Our defence of the innocent unborn... needs to be clear, firm and passionate, for at stake is the dignity of a human life, which is always sacred and demands love for each person, regardless of his or her stage of development. Equally sacred, however, are the lives of the poor, those already born, the destitute, the abandoned and the underprivileged, the vulnerable infirm and elderly exposed to covert euthanasia, the victims of human trafficking, new forms of slavery, and every form of rejection. We cannot uphold an ideal of holiness that would ignore injustice...

Pope Francis, Gaudete et Exsultate[23]

A prayer for refugees, asylum seekers and migrants

We wept when we saw the little boy
lying face down in the surf,
lifted so carefully in the arms
of the tall, bewildered police officer.
In one life, one image, the pain of millions
was captured and we cramped
with pity, determined to open our hearts
and our doors to those who gave everything
to clamber into dinghies and trucks
to get away from the shelling, the grinding, dusty poverty,
to find what we call normal –
undestroyed neighbourhoods, the morning commute, food on the table.

Lord, help us to be honest with ourselves
and with each other,
as the tide turns,
and some believe we have gone too far
in welcoming the stranger,
and some would close the gates
and build a wall,
and see nothing but threat.
Are we really open to the refugee, the migrant,
those who seek asylum at our border,
or is the prayer in our heart
that they be housed and cared for, Lord,
but just not on my street,
or at my table?

Lord, give us open hearts,
and honest hearts,
hearts that can see
how far we often are from welcoming you
into our midst.
Don't give up on us.
Don't turn from our door.

Where is the crib of Bethlehem today? Where might we find the infant Christ to worship? In many places, admittedly in every delivery room and nursery in the world, but "preferentially" in refugee camps; in boats making perilous journeys across the Mediterranean; in migrants trekking endless miles in hunger, thirst, and dangerous conditions; in people waiting in endless lines to be processed in hope of being accepted somewhere, in persons arriving at various borders after a long journey only to be sent back; in mothers in detention centers, holding their young and hoping; and most especially, preferentially, in the faces of countless refugee children.

Ronald Rolheiser, "The Christ-Child of the Year"[24]

When my child is asleep[25]

Lord, as I gaze upon this child sleeping peacefully, I feel inadequate.
Can I rise to the challenge of loving them into adulthood?
Please help me to:

Give this child reasons to believe I am trustworthy.
Offer this child more time than luxuries.
Teach this child why something is wrong rather
    than giving them a rule.
Give this child the words "please,"
    "thank you" and "sorry" and use them.
Paint this child a lasting memory of me smiling.
Be courageous enough to say "no" sometimes
    so this child feels safe.
Teach hope and patience by not giving them
    everything they want.
Show this child the hurt they can cause
    so that they learn to be compassionate.
Demonstrate pleasure in the ordinary things
    so that they feel easily content.
Talk naturally to you in front of them
    so that they learn how to pray.
Show them how easy it is to pick up litter
    rather than complaining about it.
Care for other people so that they learn to be just.
Allow them to grow up at their pace
    so they learn to enjoy themselves.
Give them enough freedom not to feel afraid of the world.
Navigate social media with them so they can make good choices.

Teach them your goodness so that they begin to enjoy you.

Respond to them with mercy first and judgment second.

Give them confidence that love brought them into the world
(even if it has failed since).

Show them that I love and respect their grandparents.

When I fail to be the parent I should be, forgive me, guide me
and inspire me to do better.

Thank you for the trust you have placed in giving us this
child, your gift to our lives.

Amen.

> Each new life "allows us to appreciate the utterly gratuitous
> dimension of love, which never ceases to amaze us. It is the beauty
> of being loved first: children are loved even before they arrive."
> Here we see a reflection of the primacy of the love of God, who
> always takes the initiative, for children "are loved before having
> done anything to deserve it."
>
> Pope Francis, *Amoris Laetitia* ("The Joy of Love")[26]

Personal reflection

- What does it mean to love your child?

- What does the love of a parent look like, sound like and act like?

When new life comes

Should God give me the days, I pray I remember...

to push you around the garden in that stupid yellow car
again and again and again, because for some reason
that only you and no one else in the world can fathom,
it makes you laugh.

Should God give me the days, I pray I remember...

to call you up and tell you that even though you came fourth
you did better than I could, that your victory will come,
and that you shouldn't be upset,
because most people don't win the first time.

Should God give me the days, I pray I remember...

when I see you one day walking towards me
laughing with your friends like nothing could ever touch you,
to step discreetly aside, knowing that now is
not the time to stop you and ask how your exams went.

Should God give me the days, I pray I remember...

that wherever we are in the world, you and I,
finding you on your twenty-first birthday was worth
the trip, just to tell you how fantastic you look,
aware that those young eyes have more power in them
than you will ever know or understand.

Should God give me the days, I pray I remember...

to tell you to pray before you decide, knowing that
God has given you the most dangerous of all gifts, freedom.
The freedom to disagree; the freedom to choose your path,
and the freedom to walk it with whom you prefer.

Should God give me the days, I pray I remember...

when I'm really old (even older than I am now)
to tell you that I was there at the beginning of it all,
to welcome you to life, when your grandma held you
and for one brief moment time stood still;
and you, of all of us, had no idea at all what was going on.

> I thank my God every time I remember you, constantly praying
> with joy in every one of my prayers for all of you, because of
> your sharing in the gospel from the first day until now. I am
> confident of this, that the one who began a good work among
> you will bring it to completion by the day of Jesus Christ.
>
> Philippians 1:3-6

Personal reflection

- When do you stop and take the long view?

- Why is it good to love people for a long time?

A prayer for our children

Lord, thank you for the lives of our children.
Thank you for the gift of their being.
Thank you for the humility
their arrival brought into our lives,
when we were pushed from the centre of our own concerns
and really learned what it meant to love,
to seek the good of another.

Help us now to let go,
just as we let them go to the park for the first time,
and then into town to meet a friend, and then to university,
where they could get a tattoo, eat junk food, date who they liked.
We want to be there for them;
we can't bear to think of them heartbroken, at risk,
or lonely in some drab place.
But to love them is to let them grow, let them go
to follow their star, their mission, their crazy dreams,
as Mary and Joseph knew only too well,
as every parent knows.
Look after them, Lord;
keep them always in your loving care.

When the festival was ended and they started to return, the boy Jesus stayed behind in Jerusalem, but his parents did not know it. Assuming that he was in the group of travellers, they went a day's journey. Then they started to look for him among their relatives and friends. When they did not find him, they returned to Jerusalem to search for him. After three days they found him in the temple, sitting among the teachers, listening to them and asking them questions. And all who heard him were amazed at his understanding and his answers. When his parents saw him they were astonished; and his mother said to him, "Child, why have you treated us like this? Look, your father and I have been searching for you in great anxiety." He said to them, "Why were you searching for me? Did you not know that I must be in my Father's house?" But they did not understand what he said to them. Then he went down with them and came to Nazareth, and was obedient to them. His mother treasured all these things in her heart.

Luke 2:43-51

When love chooses you

Born into a simple family, a carpenter's apprentice.
Born to an illiterate teenage mother with no A plus grades.
Born to refugees with no known address.
Born into a trough the animals ate out of,
    in a room to house animals with bovine TB.
Born under military rule,
    violently imposed by a narcissist who murdered babies.
Growing up in a forgotten corner.
It could have been a New York, or a New Orleans,
    Saint Boniface or St. John's, but it wasn't.
God chose a troubled first-century Palestine.

Foretold by prophets, who spoke of a face spat at, of his clothes
    becoming a prize in a game played by the bullies who murdered him.
Foretold by a man who lived on honey, who ate insects and who
    shouted at the crowds.
Foretold by his cousin, who was beheaded with a machete, whose
    head would be paraded around like something off a perverse
    YouTube video.
Foretold by his Father, who poured love upon him from the skies.
Feared by evil, tempted by wealth, power and glory, isolated and
    alone in the desert.
He could have had a media campaign, celebrity endorsements and
    corporate sponsorship.
But he didn't.
God chose a man who wore camel skins to prepare his campaign.

He picked fishermen, prone to anger and unreliability,
tax collectors, the most unpopular of men,
James and John, who harboured career ambitions.

He chose a doubter, who couldn't trust what Jesus said until he could see it for himself.

A political activist, who would go behind his back, betray him and then run away.

He chose friends who argued among themselves, vied for attention, fell asleep when he most needed them, and who denied him as he bled to death.

He could have gone after people of influence: doctors, professors, theologians, lawyers and entrepreneurs. But he didn't.

God chose those who were unqualified and unprepared.

He set about healing those who were reviled and despised.

After he met them,

paralyzed people walked away from people's indignation,

lepers returned to their families.

He freed those possessed by voices of self-loathing.

Those who were blind and deaf, the withered and broken, he restored anyone who was cast out.

Even death's sting retreated from him. He could have stayed with the teachers and elders he impressed in the temple as a little boy. But he didn't.

He chose the broken people, those who were dirty or lonely, and he proved to them that no one was beyond the love of his Father.

He taught with authority because he lived perfectly what he said.

When hunger threatened them, he transformed the little they gave him.

When fear of drowning threatened to destroy them, he calmed their storm.

When their religion became proper but loveless, he dared to challenge it.

He told them parables which held up a mirror to their souls and when they looked in it they made plans to kill him.

He could have ridden into Jerusalem on a stallion.
He could have chosen an Aston Martin or Porsche.
But he didn't.
He chose a donkey.

Betrayed by a friend, denied by his disciples,
abandoned in Gethsemane,
accused by false witnesses,
tried by corrupt lawyers,
sentenced by a coward,
jeered at by the crowds,
pitied by the daughters of Rachel,
tortured to death by a brutal army.
He could have raised an army from the stones.
He could have chosen the way of the sword.
But he didn't.
He chose silence to reply to his accuser, and he chose the cup his Father
gave him to drink.

He transformed the world forever with one word: "Mary," he said, and
she knew in that moment that the world would never be the same.
He walked with those who were depressed on the road and their
hearts burst into flames of joy.
He appeared to Thomas and gave him the evidence his logic longed for.
There will be an end to tears of sorrow.
Death is no longer the end.
Now there would always be hope for the world.
He could have returned angry with the world, to seek revenge for all
the wrong they did to him.
But he didn't.
He chose forgiveness, showed us his hands and his side and then he
offered us his peace.

Who will be his disciples now?

God can choose those who are successful, powerful and popular. But supposing none of that really impresses God at all. Supposing everything they ever achieved was his gift anyway. Suppose that today, God is choosing you. Suppose that who Jesus lived for, who he stood for, who he died for, and who he rose again for, is you. Suppose his loving Father is your loving Father, and suppose he loves you, just as you are, so that you would never have to prove yourself. To anyone. Ever again. Young women and men of the Church, today love chooses you.

In the words of Pope Francis, I invite you all, at this very moment, to a renewed personal encounter with Jesus Christ.

Lord, it is not enough to know about you: come into my life. Choose me.

Amen.

> I invite all Christians, everywhere, at this very moment, to a renewed personal encounter with Jesus Christ, or at least an openness to letting him encounter them; I ask all of you to do this unfailingly each day. No one should think that this invitation is not meant for him or her, since "no one is excluded from the joy brought by the Lord."
>
> Pope Francis, *Evangelii Gaudium*[27]

Personal reflection

- What is the difference between knowing about Jesus and meeting him?

- How do you respond to an invitation to meet Jesus?

Repent/change your mind

I used to think "repenting" was about being sorry for my sins
and then doing "penance"
to be right again with God –
a few Hail Marys, nothing too arduous –
until the next stumble, which resembled the last stumble.
I *was* sorry for my sins and sorry the next time as well,
but never really felt that much was changing, that I was changing.
The operating system was the same.

Lord, whatever word you used in your mother tongue,
those who remembered your first message in public
used the Greek word *metanoia* – meaning change, a change of mind,
or mindset, the way you look at things.
That makes more sense to me than the carousel of repentance.
Give me the grace to know where to start
with a new mind.

> Now after John was arrested, Jesus came to Galilee,
> proclaiming the good news of God, and saying,
> "The time is fulfilled, and the kingdom of God has
> come near; repent, and believe in the good news."
>
> Mark 1:14-15

> To repent is not to take on afflictive penances like fasting,
> vigils, flagellation, or whatever else appeals to your generosity.
> It means *to change the direction in which you are looking for
> happiness*. This challenge goes to the root of the problem.
>
> Thomas Keating, *Invitation to Love*[28]

49

◆ When the party goes wrong

When listening and learning become shouting and snarling:
Lord, turn our water into wine.

When curiosity and openness become prejudice and discrimination:
Lord, turn our water into wine.

When vision and daring become regulated and suffocated:
Lord, turn our water into wine.

When hope and courage become cynicism and fear:
Lord, turn our water into wine.

When big people start talking small:
Lord, turn our water into wine.

When vocation and service become advantage and privilege:
Lord, turn our water into wine.

When our smile becomes freeze-framed and stuck in place:
Lord, turn our water into wine.

When saving for a comfortable future replaces a happy now:
Lord, turn our water into wine.

When humility and gentleness become reputation and standing:
Lord, turn our water into wine.

When it all slowly and bewilderingly becomes about us
   and not about you:
   Lord, turn our water into wine.

With the confidence of your mother at Cana,
we look to you in all our human weakness,
our worldwide banquet not quite working out as it should,
and we pray,
fill us, jars of dirty water,
with new wine and teach us to bring joy to the celebration.

Amen.

> When the wine gave out, the mother of Jesus said to him,
> "They have no wine." And Jesus said to her, "Woman, what
> concern is that to you and to me? My hour has not yet come."
> His mother said to the servants, "Do whatever he tells you."
>
> John 2:3-5

Personal reflection

- When do you notice that things that
  should be joyful have become joyless?

When I want to give up

Jesus…

When I'm bored you say,
 "Follow me, and I'll make you fishers of people."

When I worry you say,
 "Your heavenly Father knows what you need."

When I have given up you say,
 "Cast your nets on the other side."

When I'm falling behind you say,
 "The last shall be first."

When I feel guilty and ashamed you say,
 "Go in peace, your sins are forgiven."

When I don't know where to go you say,
 "Abide in me."

When I want to avoid growing up you say,
 "Pick up your cross and follow me."

When I'm deceitful you say,
 "Hurry, I need to eat with you today."

When rejection paralyzes me you say,
 "Shake the dust off your feet."

When I feel intimidated you say,
 "The least among you is the greatest."

When I run from responsibility you say,
 "Give them something to eat yourself."

When I rely on my strength you say,
 "I'm sending you out like a lamb."

When I'm confused about the future you say,
 "Come and see."

When I have a falling out with people you say,
 "Love one another as I love you."

When I feel unworthy you say,
 "I call you friends."

When I avoid the poor you say,
  "You did it to me."
When I can't grasp it you say,
  "Welcome the kingdom of God like a child."
When I'm weary you say,
  "I will give you rest."
When I feel worthless you say,
  "Every hair on your head has been counted."
When my plans don't work you say,
  "Trust in God, trust in me."
When my prayer seems useless you say,
  "Seek and you will find."
When I doubt you say,
  "Here, put your finger in my side."
When I deny I have met you, you say,
  "Do you love me?"
When I abandon you for an easier life you say,
  "Father, forgive them."
When I don't know what to do you say,
  "I'll send you my Spirit."

Lord, help me not to give up, the way you never give up on us.

Amen.

> For God so loved the world that he gave his
> only Son, so that everyone who believes in
> him may not perish but may have eternal life.
>
> John 3:16

Personal reflection

- Which of the responses of Jesus give you life today?

◆ When Jesus asks the questions

What is your name?   (Be careful not to
What is it that you want?   answer too quickly)
Why do you involve me?
What do you want me to do for you?
Why do you call me "good"?

Why are you afraid?
Why do you worry?
Why did you doubt?
Where is your faith?

Are your hearts hardened?

Who do you say that I am?
Will you give me a drink?
Do you want to get well?
Do you see anything?
Do you understand what I have done for you?

Have I not chosen you?
Do you want to leave too?
Who is it that you are looking for?
Have you any fish?
Do you love me?

20 questions Jesus asks in the Gospels (there are others).

Personal reflection

• Can you allow Jesus to ask you these questions today?

• What is your reply?

When reading the Gospels

Lord, it is one thing to read but another to see and another to hear it. May we go beyond the words and may the words take us beyond ourselves.

To have seen the look of excitement when the fishermen realized they were coming with you.

To have listened to the silence of those salt-hardened seafarers as they stepped ashore, realizing that the mighty waves were subject to your command.

To have sat somewhere near the back observing over the heads of those in front the way a room went quiet when you told your stories. What a privilege to have seen the light of the campfire on your face when the story became a knife cutting its way into the very hearts of your listeners.

To have observed the perplexity on their faces when they realized that all their scheming, plotting and invention could not trap you. To have witnessed their confusion when you neither fought them nor ran away, but stood before them radiant with integrity.

To have seen the look on his face when you stopped short and called up into that sycamore tree: "Zacchaeus. Hurry. I must eat with you tonight."

To have witnessed the glance your mother gave you when she caught your eye across a crowded room in Cana, she alone knowing who had called forth the finest wines.

I'd have liked to have witnessed the woman who met you at Jacob's well, running like a child into her village; or the centurion awestruck before his healed servant; or the woman rising out of the dust as her accusers dropped their stones.

What look of wounded love must have distorted your mother's stricken face, who saw you learn your trade, and now stood before you as you were crushed under timber, of all things, on the cruel, unforgiving road to Golgotha.

What look of wonderment must have lit up Mary Magdalene's face, when grief-stricken, doubled over and pitiful, she heard her name called in love and knew in an instant it was you who spoke to her from among the graves.

Could Thomas bear to raise his gaze to yours when invited, by the voice who first called him, to put his finger in your side?

Lord, give us eyes to see and ears to hear. May we go beyond the words and may the words take us beyond ourselves.

Amen.

> But blessed are your eyes, for they see, and your ears, for they hear. Truly I tell you, many prophets and righteous people longed to see what you see, but did not see it, and to hear what you hear, but did not hear it.
>
> Matthew 13:16-17

Personal reflection

- Read a few of the Gospel stories where people meet Jesus.

- Try to imagine the faces, as well as listen to the words they say.

- What do you see?

When I meet someone homeless and poor, what do I do?

He knew from far out he'd caught my eye –
early twenties, sitting on the pavement, cap in front of him –
we both said later he looked like our middle son,
the one who's back home, the one
who needs a bit more of us –
"Spare any change, man?"
"What about some food, can I get you some food?"
"Prefer the money, man, get me a roof for the night."
"Sure, no problem, there you go. Take care."
"Cheers, man, that's rare. Have a good evening."
"You too, now."

Just around the corner there was another man
on the pavement, cap in hand – "Spare any change?" –
But this one we did not recognize and, besides,
you can't help everybody, can you?
"No, sorry. I've got no change."
"You have a good evening, buddy."
I walked on, fingering the change in my pocket.

Lord, help me to know
what to do when I meet people
who ask outright for help.
Help me to get over the calculations of the heart –
do they look genuine, will it just go on drugs,
should I give to a charity instead?

Lord, help me to recognize the need,
and know the right thing to do.
Help me to know you
when I see you.

Truly I tell you, just as you did not do it to one of the least of these,
you did not do it to me.

Matthew 25:45

To be truly spiritual people in our own time, rote religion will not
do. Only by applying the Word of God to the issues of the day can
we ever hope to claim to be disciples now. The issues we face now
confront every value the Gospel preaches. Immigration, poverty
and equality test the very reality of discipleship. How do we
practice hospitality in a global world where the destitute refugee
has followed the cash crops taken from her own country to the
garbage cans of this one?

Joan Chittister, In God's Holy Light[29]

The problem is not feeding the poor, or clothing the naked or
visiting the sick, but rather recognizing that the poor, the naked,
the sick, prisoners and the homeless have the dignity to sit at our
table, to feel "at home" among us, to feel part of a family. This is
the sign that the kingdom of heaven is in our midst. This is the
sign of a Church wounded by sin, shown mercy by the Lord, and
made prophetic by his call.

Pope Francis, Evangelii Gaudium[30]

If I can stop one heart from breaking,
I shall not live in vain;
If I can ease one life the aching,
Or cool one pain,
Or help one fainting robin
Unto his nest again,
I shall not live in vain.

Emily Dickinson, "If I Can Stop One Heart from Breaking"[31]

On learning to slow down and encounter people

(Andrew is a friend with Down syndrome)

At the end of Mass I wouldn't touch the sides on the way out. For that matter, I wouldn't touch the sides on the way in: my mind was full of the week ahead, the long "to do" list, the conversations I needed to have, the arguments I needed to win. "Go in peace…" was like a starter pistol; I was out of the blocks and out of sight. Until I met Andrew and started taking him to Mass.

Leaving quickly was not an option. After Mass, we had to go to the hall for tea and Andrew had to speak to *everybody*. "Hi, I'm Andrew," he'd say, extending a hand and a smile. To begin with, I could not cope with this pace. My teeth were on edge. I'd be at his elbow, encouraging him to finish his tea and go. But Andrew had other ideas and I soon gave up on trying to hurry him along. And then, one Sunday, the penny dropped. My God, so that's how you do it, I thought. The people you've raced past all this time you just *talk* to. You take your time, you take Andrew's time, you ask people how they're doing and then, when you're good and ready, you make a leisurely exit, with one final chat on the way out.

Lord, slow us down.
Help us to take time to be with people,
to be really present to them,
to take part in the sacrament of encounter
with grace and patience.

Thank you for our friends with intellectual disabilities, who teach us that time is a glimpse of eternity,
that in the eyes of the poor,
if we have eyes to see,
we see you.

Now as they went on their way, he entered a certain village, where a woman named Martha welcomed him into her home. She had a sister named Mary, who sat at the Lord's feet and listened to what he was saying. But Martha was distracted by her many tasks; so she came to him and asked, "Lord, do you not care that my sister has left me to do all the work by myself? Tell her then to help me." But the Lord answered her, "Martha, Martha, you are worried and distracted by many things; there is need of only one thing. Mary has chosen the better part, which will not be taken away from her."

Luke 10:38-42

These broken, wounded, and completely unpretentious people forced me to let go of my relevant self – the self that can do things, show things, prove things, build things – and forced me to reclaim that unadorned self in which I am completely vulnerable, open to receive and give love regardless of any accomplishments.

Henri Nouwen, *In the Name of Jesus*[32]

Being with Jesus means being in the company of the people whose company Jesus seeks and keeps. Jesus chooses the company of the excluded, the disreputable, the wretched, the self-hating, the poor, the diseased; so that is where you are going to find yourself. If you are going to be where Jesus is, if your discipleship is not intermittent but a way of being, you will find yourself in the same sort of company as he is in. It is once again a reminder that our discipleship is not about choosing our company but choosing the company of Jesus – or rather, getting used to the fact of having been chosen for the company of Jesus.

Rowan Williams, *Being Disciples*[33]

It may be possible for each to think too much of his own potential glory hereafter; it is hardly possible for him to think too often or too deeply about that of his neighbour. The load, or weight, or burden of my neighbour's glory should be laid on my back, a load so heavy that only humility can carry it, and the backs of the proud will be broken.

C. S. Lewis, *The Weight of Glory*[34]

Personal reflection

- When was the last time I consciously slowed down and allowed myself to "waste time" in ordinary encounters?

- What do I see when I see a person with an intellectual disability?

- Would I benefit from seeking out the company of those with an intellectual disability?

Who am I?

After a disturbing dream

My child,
You are not your dreams.
You are not your moods.
You are not your thoughts.

You are not your "likes."
You are not your followers.
You are not your friends.

You are not what others see,
or say,
or think.

You are not your grades.
You are not your personal best.
You are not your salary.

You are not your data.
You are not your body measurements.
You are not your looks.

You are so much more.
Your deepest you
is beauty beyond comprehension.

You are a temple
where I am pleased to dwell.
If you open
the door.

O LORD, you have searched me and known me.
You know when I sit down and when I rise up;
you discern my thoughts from far away.
You search out my path and my lying down,
and are acquainted with all my ways.
Even before a word is on my tongue,
O LORD, you know it completely.

Psalm 139:1-4

My deepest me is God.

St Catherine of Genoa

Thus it is that the holy synod proclaims the noble calling of humanity and the existence within it of a divine seed.

Second Vatican Council, Gaudium et Spes
(Pastoral Constitution on the Church in the Modern World)[35]

How wonderful is the certainty that each human life is not adrift in the midst of hopeless chaos, in a world ruled by pure chance or endlessly recurring cycles! The Creator can say to each one of us: "Before I formed you in the womb, I knew you"... We were conceived in the heart of God, and for this reason "each of us is the result of a thought of God. Each of us is willed, each of us is loved, each of us is necessary."

Pope Francis, Laudato Si' (On Care for Our Common Home)[36]

◆ When I lose my faith

Growing up,
we were inspired by the martyrs
who had "kept the faith" in spite of dungeon, fire and sword.
Faith of our fathers.
It was something you believed and didn't deny,
even if somebody was pulling your body apart.
At times, it mysteriously vanished,
like when that priest "lost his faith" and was never seen again.
It seemed like a huge body of knowledge
that we had to keep agreeing to, whether we understood it or not.
But that's not what the Gospel seems to be saying.
There, it's more like a person, who presents themselves to Jesus
with a big, open, desperate heart
as if to say, "It's over to you now; please help me."
And they're saved, made well in mind and body,
and sometimes they don't even have to sign up for the team.
Go, your faith has made you well.

Lord, help me to see
when the eyes of faith are dimmed
and my heart is hardened
by the ordinary obsessions of the world,
by the tiredness that sets in over the years,
the cynicism that sees bad intentions everywhere,
when it becomes easier
just to look after my own, my little nest,
and arrange my pleasures around me
because I "deserve" them.

Help me to open up to you in faith,

like the wayward son who has come to his senses,

to come back home with my heart wide open,

knowing that there's nothing I can do to impress you,

   to earn this grace.

All is gift, even the very desire to come to you,

the first stirring of the search for you,

is your Spirit in me.

Lord, touch me with your presence, make me well,

make me know your forgiveness,

the grace of your life, the amazing grace

which would blind me and save me,

if only I had the simple faith

to let you in.

> Then Jesus said to him, "What do you want me to do for you?" The blind man said to him, "My teacher, let me see again." Jesus said to him, "Go; your faith has made you well." Immediately he regained his sight and followed him on the way.
>
> Mark 10:51-52

> We do not believe in formulas, but in those realities they express, which faith allows us to touch. "The believer's act [of faith] does not terminate in the propositions, but in the realities [which they express]." All the same, we do approach these realities with the help of formulations of the faith which permit us to express the faith and to hand it on, to celebrate it in community, to assimilate and live on it more and more.
>
> *Catechism of the Catholic Church*, 170

Faith says that God is real and God is Lord and, because of this, there is ultimately nothing to fear. We are in safe hands. Reality is gracious, forgiving, loving, redeeming, and absolutely trustworthy. Our task is to surrender to that.

Ronald Rolheiser, Prayer[37]

The Church has repeatedly taught that we are justified not by our own works or efforts, but by the grace of the Lord, who always takes the initiative. The Fathers of the Church, even before Saint Augustine, clearly expressed this fundamental belief. Saint John Chrysostom said that God pours into us the very source of all his gifts even before we enter into battle.

Pope Francis, Gaudete et Exsultate[38]

Personal reflection

- What or who do I have faith in?

- Am I able to approach the living God with faith, open to the life of grace freely given?

- Do I recognize that "all is gift," even the desire to come closer to God?

When I'm losing purpose[39]

You are the reason he chose his disciples.

You are the reason he went from village to village.

You are the reason he ate with sinners and outcasts.

You are the reason he picked corn on the sabbath.

You are the reason he set his face like flint to Jerusalem.

You are the reason he offered himself as bread broken for the world.

You are the reason he did not give into his fear in the Garden of
  Gethsemane.

You are the reason he offered no resistance when the soldiers came
  to arrest him.

You are the reason he did not resent betrayal by his closest friends.

You are the reason he let them spit on him and dress him to be
  laughed at.

You are the reason he stood resilient before a jeering crowd.

You are the reason he stayed silent before his accusers.

You are the reason he remained dignified while they beat him almost
  to death.

You are the reason he picked up his cross.

You are the reason he carried it to his place of execution.

You are the reason he did not give up, even when they pushed
  nails into his wrists.

You are the reason he forgave as he prayed to his father from
  the cross.

You are the reason he gave up his last breath.

Yours is the life he dignified. You are his reason to love.

Lord, when I can't remember why I am and who I am, be my reason.

Be my reason to get out of bed.

Be my reason to lift my gaze.

Be my reason to sing.

Be my reason to cheer up.

Be my reason to love first.

Be my reason to be grateful.

Be my reason to continue.

Be my reason to be courageous.

Be my reason to walk into an unknown future.

Be my reason to rise above the things which diminish me.

Be my reason to resist the gossip and the politics of self-preservation.

Be my reason to enjoy my life when others complain about theirs.

Be my reason to believe when others use your name as a swear word.

Be my reason to forgive when other people condemn.

Be my reason to welcome people before I judge.

Be my reason to know that my life is not useless or worthless,
    but full of possibility.

Be my reason to dance the dance.

Lord, you made me your reason from the moment you emerged from
    the River Jordan.

Be my reason today.

Amen.

> There is no fear in love, but perfect love casts out fear; for fear
> has to do with punishment, and whoever fears has not reached
> perfection in love. We love because he first loved us.
>
> 1 John 4:18-19

Personal reflection

- Can we draw upon the love we have received to give in kind?

In praise of creation

Lord, it is good to be here,
on the good earth, our common home.
What you made is holy. Praise to you, Lord, for creation,
for the morning sun, the ripening fruit,
the oceans rolling in splendour, the life-giving trees,
the animals at play in the wilderness, the glancing shoals of fish:
grace-filled, charged with grandeur.
Help us to be good dwellers on this earth,
to look after what has been entrusted to us from all eternity,
to live more simply and not to aspire to a lifestyle
that cannot be shared by all.
Help us to be attentive to what we consume, where it comes from,
the impact of its production.
Give us the grace to be open to reality,
to hear the cries of pain from the sea, the shanty towns,
the steaming landfills where children pick over toxic waste for a living.
Let us be aware of who we are in the scheme of things: your hands,
to till and tend the goods of creation,
to be shared among everybody;
your creatures, grateful
for the gift of life.

> So God created humankind in his image,
> in the image of God he created them;
> male and female he created them.
> God blessed them, and God said to them, "Be fruitful and multiply,
> and fill the earth and subdue it; and have dominion over the fish of
> the sea and over the birds of the air and over every living thing that
> moves upon the earth."
>
> Genesis 1:27-28

70

Consider the lilies of the field, how they grow; they
neither toil nor spin, yet I tell you, even Solomon
in all his glory was not clothed like one of these.

Matthew 6:28-29

Earth's crammed with heaven,
And every common bush afire with God;
But only he who sees, takes off his shoes,
The rest sit round it and pluck
blackberries.

Elizabeth Barrett Browning, from "Aurora Leigh"[40]

The pale flowers of the dogwood outside this window are saints.
The little yellow flowers that nobody notices on the edge of that
road are saints looking up into the face of God. This leaf has its own
texture and its own pattern of veins and its own holy shape, and the
bass and trout hiding in the deep pools of the river are canonized
by their beauty and their strength. The lakes hidden among the
hills are saints, and the sea too is a saint who praises God without
interruption in her majestic dance.

Thomas Merton, *New Seeds of Contemplation*[41]

To blame population growth instead of extreme and selective
consumerism on the part of some, is one way of refusing to face
the issues. It is an attempt to legitimize the present model of
distribution, where a minority believes that it has the right to
consume in a way which can never be universalized, since the planet
could not even contain the waste products of such consumption.

Pope Francis, *Laudato Si'*[42]

When the future of our world scares me[43]

O Lord my God, when I in awesome wonder,
   consider all the worlds thy hands have made;
I see the stars, I hear the rolling thunder,
   thy power throughout the universe displayed.
O Lord my God...

Climatologists tell us that we are destroying our common home.

Economists tell us we're not going to have enough savings for our old age.

Traders tell us we're falling behind in the global race for prosperity.

Nutritionists tell us we're eating ourselves into diabetes.

Business analysts tell us that children will be worse off than their parents.

Ecologists tell us forests will have to be protected by force.

IT gurus tell us that our personal details will be vulnerable.

Biologists tell us that we'll respond poorly to antibiotics.

Oceanographers tell us we're consuming plastic through the food chain.

Engineers tell us robots will replace us at work.

Meteorologists tell us to expect "extreme weather."

Religious leaders tell us we're losing our moral compass.

Sociologists tell us we're losing touch with each other.

Psychiatrists tell us mental illness is escalating.

Educationalists tell us we'll know a little about everything and not a lot about anything.

What am I to do with this? So much lies beyond my control.

Lord, may I never give in to complacency about the future of our world, and at the same time help me to trust in your providence. May I be motivated by the urgency of these issues but not enslaved by despair or cynicism. I entrust to you, almighty and loving God, all that is good and beautiful and, when I have done what is to be done, help me to sleep the sleep of saints so that I am ready to begin again tomorrow. Thank you for the beauty and abundance in creation. May we learn how to enjoy it the way you meant us to.

Amen.

> Creating a world in need of development, God in some way sought to limit himself in such a way that many of the things we think of as evils, dangers or sources of suffering, are in reality part of the pains of childbirth which he uses to draw us into the act of cooperation with the Creator.
>
> Pope Francis, *Laudato Si'*[44]

Personal reflection

• What does it mean to cooperate with the creator?

When things aren't just right

Thank you for the dappled things.

For terms and conditions in tiny print.
For indecipherable contracts and bullet points.
For huge instruction manuals in twenty languages.
For insider terminology and technical jargon.

Thank you for the dappled things.

For bag handles which break.
For narrow parking spaces.
For the times they move the products around.
For missing parts in flat-pack furniture.

Thank you for the dappled things.

For glitches in "communication."
For jammed feeder trays in busy copiers.
For servers going down.
For reports diligently written which no one reads.

Thank you for the dappled things.

For grey days with a chance of rain.
For spots and wrinkles.
For getting sick while on vacation.
For dead car batteries on cold mornings.

Thank you for the dappled things.

For lost pin numbers and forgotten passwords.
For certificates we can't find.
For warranties and guarantees we thought were in a drawer.

Thank you for the dappled things.

For Mondays.
For bosses in a hurry.
For data reviews and deadlines.
For targets and performance reviews.

Thank you for the dappled things.

Because, in the end, Lord, it is right and just
to give you thanks, always and everywhere.

Amen.

> Glory be to God for dappled things –
>
> ... All things counter, original, spare, strange;
>   Whatever is fickle, freckled (who knows how?)
>   With swift, slow; sweet, sour; adazzle, dim;
> He fathers-forth whose beauty is past change:
>   Praise him.
>
> Gerard Manley Hopkins, "Pied Beauty"[45]

Personal reflection

• Why might gratitude be so important?

When I start complaining too much

Dear Jesus,

I am not in a crowd, I am the crowd.
I am not waiting in a queue, I am the queue.
I am not stuck in traffic, I am the traffic.
I am not in a culture, I am the culture.
I am not in this community, I am this community.
I am not in an environment, I am the environment.
I am not in a church, I am the Church.

Help me to stop waiting for everyone else
to get out of my way.

Help me to stop waiting for everyone else
to change.

Help me to stop waiting for someone else
to sort it out.

Help me to stop complaining and start the healing,
no matter how small the gesture.

Help me to move from watching you to becoming you.
And as I do so, walk beside me every step, to stop me
falling back into blah blah blah whine whine whine
blame blame blame complain complain complain.

Save me from the disease of complaining a lot and doing little. By your grace, prevent me sleepwalking into an early grave. Restore the smile you gave me (on the inside and the outside) and then propel me out of my easy chair of judgment.

Gratefully yours forever.

Amen.

> Why do you see the speck in your neighbour's eye, but do not notice the log in your own eye? Or how can you say to your neighbour, "Let me take the speck out of your eye," while the log is in your own eye? You hypocrite, first take the log out of your own eye, and then you will see clearly to take the speck out of your neighbour's eye.
>
> Matthew 7:3-5

Personal reflection

- What is the best antidote for an addiction to complaining?

When I'm running on an empty battery

Lord, these days almost everything needs to be plugged into a power supply. My phone needs power, my laptop needs power and all around me people are looking for sockets in the wall. The entire hall I sit in is ablaze with bright light. I'm surrounded by sockets and wires hidden in the walls. This relentless power lights up everything but me.

Meanwhile my own power is draining. My spirit weakens, my strength is diminished. I grow hungry, thirsty, restless. I'm slowly draining, emptying out, slowing down. It doesn't take much, Lord. The hurt I feel, the pain I see, makes me feel empty.

Revive my drooping spirit, Lord. Ignite me with your fire. Quench my thirst. Nourish me with your bread. Raise my gaze. Revive my smile. Strengthen these limbs. Breathe your power supply into these fragile lungs, that I may be an athlete on this pilgrimage.

Rise up, you tired and weary bones. Subside, you thoughts of limitation and constraint. Fall away, you garment of sorrow and affliction.

Lord, may my thoughts of powerlessness turn to those around me who are powerless. Fill me with your strength, that they may see me in your light and plug instead into you.

Amen.

I am confident of this, that the one who began a good work among you will bring it to completion by the day of Jesus Christ.

Philippians 1:6

On the need for sabbath rest

Lord, the list of things I've got to do is long.
I know it's Sunday, but if I don't clear the backlog it'll pile up.
I work hard, I support my family, I put in the hours.
I convince myself that this is virtuous.
It's not wrong, is it?
No, it's just not what you told us from the beginning.
It says that the act of creation tired you –
after the effort of imagining life into existence
you needed to rest, to be refreshed, restored.
And so do we.

Lord, help us to see
the need to rest, to rest in you,
to gather and recover ourselves, the selves
you intended us to be on this earth, in tune with creation, with our
    neighbour,
especially our vulnerable neighbour, those in our community who
    are precarious,
the ones who are excluded from the system of success.
Help us on this holy day to look around, spend time with loved ones,
    with your word,
to gather up a different kind of energy and imagination,
to be generous and fruitful,
courageous and calm in the face of the world.

It is a sign forever between me and the people of Israel that in six days the LORD made heaven and earth, and on the seventh day he rested, and was refreshed.

Exodus 31:17

Observe the sabbath day and keep it holy, as the LORD your God commanded you. For six days you shall labour and do all your work. But the seventh day is a sabbath to the LORD your God.

Deuteronomy 5:12-14*a*

Thus the Sabbath of the fourth commandment is an act of trust in the subversive, exodus-causing God of the first commandment, an act of submission to the restful God of commandments one, two and three. Sabbath is a practical divestment so that neighbourly engagement, rather than production and consumption, defines our lives.

Walter Brueggemann, *Sabbath as Resistance*[46]

Personal reflection

- Do you have a weekly period of rest, when you turn off the pressures and anxieties of the world and seek to reconnect with God in word and sacrament, to reconnect with your neighbour and nature?

- Are you aware of how much you are "plugged in" to the empire of things, the anxiety-driven economy of competition and acquisition?

Sunday evening blues

Lord, I feel reluctance for the week ahead –
the draining commute, the demands, the routine.
Over the weekend I got a glimpse of a better life –
more time for leisure, more time
with the people who mean the most to me,
more time to do what defines me as a person.
And now, as the street lights come on
I feel a knot in my stomach
as work beckons, with meetings
I'm ill prepared for, the stress of deadlines
and the hard reality of accountability.
It feels like I live to work, not work to live.

So help me, Lord, with my reluctance –
remind me that I am not a prisoner, not homeless,
not in the grip of real poverty.
Remind me that you spent most of your life
getting up for work – hard manual work in wood and stone –
heading off with the labourers
in the cold silence of early morning, day in, day out
with just a sabbath rest to break the routine.
Remind me that in my workplace,
in all my encounters with my co-workers and the public
I can work for change, work honestly
and with a good spirit, work hard
and make the most of any opportunities to grow
and shape my work
to my vocation.

Be with me, Lord,

be with us all as we face another week,

another chance to be courageous and generous,

to step out into the storm of life,

and do good as we go.

> See, I am sending you out like sheep into the midst of wolves;
> so be wise as serpents and innocent as doves.
>
> Matthew 10:16

> Do, and dare to do, not what is arbitrary, but what is right.
> Do not linger in possibilities, bravely grasp what is real.
> Freedom does not reside in the flight of thoughts,
>   but only in action.
> Step out of fearful hesitation into the storm of events,
> supported only by God's commandment and by your faith,
> and freedom will cheerfully receive your spirit.
>
> Dietrich Bonhoeffer, *Prayers from Prison*[47]

When it's all a bit ordinary

It's a Tuesday in February. Toys strewn across the living room floor await tidying into the toy box. My wife sits next to her tepid coffee, stealing a few precious moments of reprieve in a book. Our youngest is cuddled up beside her, lost in lining up her toy figures. Our ketchup-smeared plates still sit on the table, ready for the dishwasher. The boys are arguing. There are basketball highlights on TV. It's dark outside.

So much to be grateful for. If I'm not careful I'll miss it. So perfect is this moment that, if I'm not awake, I'll get consumed by the travel brochures. For this simple Tuesday night in February, Lord, I thank you.

It's a Monday in May. A colleague shouts, "Does anyone want a coffee?" Most of us stare unflinching into our screens. There is a conversation in the far corner about counting steps. I'm interrupted by a card thrust into my hand: "Sign this," she says indignantly. "For Maureen downstairs," she adds discreetly, pointing at the floor. "It's the big five-oh. There's an envelope on my desk for a present. Don't give me coins; paper money only." She smiles as she says it, gesturing towards Geoff in the corner, who is so unwilling to share that he opens his candy in his pocket rather than offering it around. My work is done here – I am ready for the next meeting.

So much to be grateful for. If I'm not careful I'll miss it. So perfect is this moment that, if I'm not awake, I'll get consumed by performance targets and pension plans. For this simple Monday in May, Lord, I thank you.

It's a Thursday in September. Driving home after being away. It's late and the highway is empty. Seventy-four kilometres to exit 15, it says on the illuminated sign. The orange neon glistens, reflected in the super-smooth asphalt road. Everything is "smart" these days. Even the highway. Inside my roaming world, I'm consoled by music, my coffee too hot to sip, my adjustable seat adjusted. My GPS tells me I'm on the right track.

So much to be grateful for. If I'm not careful I'll miss it. So perfect is this moment that, if I'm not awake, I'll get consumed by the need to accelerate and I'll miss the journey for the sake of the destination. For this Thursday night in September, Lord, I thank you.

Lord, help me to see your glory in the Tuesdays, Mondays and Thursdays. May I learn to see your abundant grace poured out into what first seems tedious and familiar. Thank you for the breathtaking detail, so brilliant and ever-present that we can't see it. Help me to be alert not just to the special and the spectacular, but to the Tuesdays, Mondays and Thursdays... in Ordinary Time.

> Beware, keep alert; for you do not know when the time will come... And what I say to you I say to all: Keep awake.
>
> Mark 13:33, 37

Personal reflection

- What are we in danger of missing?

Before a difficult conversation

Eat the frog, is what they say –
just do the most difficult thing first
and the rest of the day, the week, will not seem so bad.
It's easier said than done, especially when I need to have *that* conversation,
the one that gives me stomach cramps.
I know I need to, I know it's right, I just know it's not going to be easy.
In truth, I'm a little afraid of the one I need to talk to.
I don't want to face their anger, their wild logic.

Lord, you didn't seem to duck those conversations.
You read our innermost thoughts and told us
when we were being hypocritical, self-serving, deluded.
You read our good intentions and knew when they weren't good enough.
You looked at us with love.
Help me to see this conversation from the other point of view –
to bring my imagination to the dialogue,
to say what has to be said, with the best words I can muster,
without losing sight of justice, without forgetting what has happened,
or what we think has happened.
Help me to be fair, considerate, clear-sighted,
to remember the human being in front of me is a child of God.

Holy Spirit, come to us both,
be with us as we struggle in the web of words and feeling,
doing our best.

> My grace is sufficient for you.
> 2 Corinthians 12:9

When the criticism is unfair

Disparaging comments, veiled criticism;
cheap words on a computer screen;
"bravery" from behind a keyboard.
That's all it may take and we are reduced.
I know that tonight when I'm in bed I'll be restless.

Face up, face down, no sleeping satisfaction.
I'll be digesting over and over this fast food for thought
     and it will bring indigestion.
Why is it that we're inclined to bow to the negatives?

Why are we not wired to see the good we can be?
Why are we blind to our own beauty,
yet see it so effortlessly in others?
Lord, increase in us.

Help me to be deaf to words of unkindness.
Help me to be blind to looks of contempt.
Help me to be thick-skinned before rejection.
Help me to stand defiant before the baying blog.
Lord, increase in me.

Help me to hear words of true wisdom.
Help me to accept loving correction.
Help me to stand defiant before the false accuser.
Help me to shake the nonsense off the soles of my shoes.
These things I can't do without you.

I must decrease, you must increase. In me.

Amen.

> He must increase, but I must decrease.
>
> John 3:30

Personal reflection

- What do I need to empty myself of, to be who God means me to be?

Before a meeting

God our Father,
we gather here today and ask for your blessing
on our work, on our thinking, on our dialogue, on our actions.
Send us your Spirit so that we may discern the better way,
mindful of the impact of our decisions,
especially on those who are most vulnerable,
and on the earth, our common home.

Help us to treat each other with respect,
so that all can have their say.
May we be magnanimous, not mean,
curious, not closed,
encouraging, not cruel.
May we let in the fresh air of humour
and good grace,
and not take ourselves too seriously.
Let us not cling to long-held opinion,
but be prepared to listen,
to change our minds,
to be surprised by insight
and new perspectives.

Let us leave room for your Spirit
to inspire,
to challenge,
to change.

We make this,
and all our prayers,
through Christ our Lord.

Amen.

Lord, I have spent months agonizing about the last few hours. Every waking moment has been spent in bizarre rehearsals, anticipating, articulating, pontificating, preparing myself for disappointment. Yet here I am, sitting in the place where I arrived this morning. A man mops the tiled floor around me. His life is just the same today as it was yesterday; not mine. Now all my adrenalin is focused on a new future. What have I done... ?

Help me to pause.

Before I call the ones I love and ask them to consider the consequences of what I'm doing; before all this accelerates; before thoughts of impending change interrupt our routine; before everything starts to look different...

Help me to pause.

Before I disappoint some and delight others; before all this becomes a phone call, a letter, an e-mail, an announcement, fumbled words of gratitude, a card from the team in the office, a discreet tear, sadness for the things I'm letting go...

Help me to pause.

Before the enormity of it all hits me; before I remember that I talked big in there, I gave confidence to others and built up hopes; before the responsibility of it all looms large; before all my promises become more human and more fragile than they sounded...

Help me to pause.

Now, Lord, as I go back home, knowing that where I came from will never be the same, knowing that going home this night is the beginning of leaving, may you walk ahead of me. Bring stillness to this unsettled water, calm to the stirring winds, and joy to the possibilities. Give peace to those who walk away from here disappointed; give courage to those I love who don't yet know; give zeal to the one who takes my place, and may I, your small, cracked earthenware pot, never forget that it was you who did all this. Before I was born.

Help me to pause.

Amen.

> During those days he went out to the mountain to pray; and he spent the night in prayer to God.
>
> Luke 6:12

Personal reflection

- When is it best to press "pause" and take time to prepare?

When I need to make my mind up

So what do I do now?
Flip a coin?
Rock, paper, scissors?
Consult a horoscope?
Ask the audience?
Phone a friend?
Google it?
Write a list of pros and cons?
Consult a business guru?
Ask people who love me?
Ask people who don't love me?
Make the decision and see how it feels in the morning?
Overthink it?
Underthink it?
Jump?
Or just stay in bed until it goes away?

Lord, I preferred it when I was a child and someone made decisions for me.

Help me to walk more by faith and less by sight. Help me to fall into my future without a parachute, a zodiac, a feel-good herbal remedy and a comfort blanket. Thank you, Lord, that whichever way I go, you'll be there ahead of me, beside me, behind me, bringing to the good all things.

> We know that all things work together for good for those who love God, who are called according to his purpose.
>
> Romans 8:28

Personal reflection

• What helps you to make strong decisions?

When I haven't finished my e-mails

They told us to sit up.
They told us to pay attention.
They told us to eat our greens.
They told us to brush our teeth.
They told us to stand in line.
They told us to wash behind our ears.
They told us to put our pens down.
They told us to try harder.
They told us to be good.
They told us to respect.
They told us to be on time.
They told us to be reliable.
They told us to be quiet.
They told us to study for the test.
They told us to make a good first impression.
They told us not to say "um" in the interview.
They told us to save for a rainy day.
They told us to meet deadlines.
They told us to be team players.
They told us to be honest.
They told us to change energy providers.
They told us to make the most of every day.
They told us to be the best we can be.
And they told us that if we work hard we'd do well in the end.
And for the most part... they were probably right.

But I must have been away the day they told us
to lighten up,
to make more mistakes,

to laugh more,

to dance when everyone's watching,

to eat cake in the sunshine,

to stop improving because it is exhausting,

to fly a kite,

to stand in the rain.

Lord, our gathered wisdom can contradict itself.

Help me to get the right things to the top of my list

and then live that way,

so that my wife gets a husband,

my children get a dad,

my colleagues get a friend,

and those who are poor get served.

And may my son never again ask me...

    "Dad, are you taking your laptop on vacation?"

Amen.

> But God said to him, "You fool! This very night
> your life is being demanded of you. And the things
> you have prepared, whose will they be?"
>
> Luke 12:20

Personal reflection

- Do the things that are important to you get the time they deserve?

- If not, what are you going to do about it?

Stressed

Lord, I don't feel so good.
I don't feel right.
Pressure is one thing.
There is pressure all the time –
    to perform, to deliver, to be successful.
But this is different.
This is a tightness in my chest,
a sudden, rising panic.
This is a night without sleep.
This is tearful, this is stress.
I am at the far end of my resources
and need help.

My child,
know that you are loved.
Rest in me awhile; lay down your burden.
I know stress, too. I know anguish.
I know what it's like to beg
that the cup will be taken away.
I have been to the worst places
that you inhabit;
in your most lonely darkness,
in your Gethsemane,
you'll find me there.

In his anguish he prayed more earnestly, and his sweat became like great drops of blood falling down on the ground.

Luke 22:44

Come to me, all you that are weary and are carrying heavy burdens, and I will give you rest. Take my yoke upon you, and learn from me; for I am gentle and humble in heart, and you will find rest for your souls. For my yoke is easy, and my burden is light.

Matthew 11:28-30

If I had a message to my contemporaries it is surely this: Be anything you like, be madmen, drunks, and bastards of every shape and form, but at all costs avoid one thing: success... If you are too obsessed with success, you will forget to live. If you have learned only how to be a success, your life has probably been wasted.

Thomas Merton, *Love and Living*[48]

Anyone who does not win feels that he is no good in this culture, whereas in the quiet of deep prayer, you are a new person, or rather, you are you.

Thomas Keating, *Open Mind, Open Heart*[49]

When did my heart get so small?

When did my heart get so small
that I stopped seeing those I love
staring me in the face when I got home at night?

When did my heart get so small
that my imagination was inspired
by success at work: another badge, or bonus, or promotion?

When did my heart get so small
that the calculations of my pension
became more important than my prayers?

When did my heart get so small
that I spent more on smart headphones
than I gave to poor people all year?

When did my heart get so small
that I stopped objecting to the high walls
around people like me,
that I ended up living on bread alone?
The bitter bread of this world:
power, prestige, possessions.

Dear Lord, on the road to Emmaus
you set fire to the hearts of your sad disciples,
sent them running back to Jerusalem with new hope.
Take my small, heavy heart: burn it up
in the great flame of your redeeming love.

The point is this: the one who sows sparingly will also reap sparingly, and the one who sows bountifully will also reap bountifully.

2 Corinthians 9:6

It is written, "One does not live by bread alone, but by every word that comes from the mouth of God."

Matthew 4:4

Batter my heart, three-person'd God, for you
As yet but knock, breathe, shine, and seek to mend;
That I may rise and stand, o'erthrow me, and bend
Your force to break, blow, burn, and make me new.

John Donne, "Batter My Heart"[50]

The person who is really alive, who isn't buried in sand while chatting away, who still feels and is touched and moved by what goes on in the world, by what happens to others, is one who runs the risk of going mad in a society that lives for bread alone and subordinates all other concerns to that of profit.

Dorothee Soelle, *Death by Bread Alone*[51]

If not now, when?

Lord, I seem to spend most of my precious time
in the future, with my endless plans
for when life will be better:
when I win the lottery,
when the mortgage is paid off,
when I'm slimmer,
when I have time to enjoy life
and lift a glass to my good fortune on the holiday of a lifetime.

Or else I'm in the past,
when things were better,
replaying the moments of triumph, the winning goal,
the sweet pleasures along the way;
or else haunted by old grievances,
memories of harm and humiliation,
stoking my unforgiveness
into a healthy bonfire.

But I'm very rarely in the *now*,
the only time I have,
where you are, the only place you can be found.
If only I could turn down the noise,
unplug my ego
and its compulsive concerns and calculations
and encounter you in the stillness
of the moment, the eternal now,
the only place to be,
the door of heaven.

So do not worry about tomorrow, for tomorrow will bring worries of its own.

Matthew 6:34

See, now is the acceptable time; see, now is the day of salvation!

2 Corinthians 6:2

The eternal present is the space within which your whole life unfolds, the one factor that remains constant. Life is now. There was never a time when your life was not now, nor will there ever be. Secondly, the Now is the only point that can take you beyond the limited confines of the mind. It is your only point of access into the timeless and formless realm of Being.

Eckhart Tolle, *The Power of Now*[52]

We should not look for heaven above the clouds. Whenever we turn to God in his glory and to our neighbor in his need; whenever we experience the joys of love; whenever we convert and allow ourselves to be reconciled with God, heaven opens there. "Not that God is where heaven is, but rather heaven is where God is."

YOUCAT: Youth Catechism of the Catholic Church[53]

Personal reflection

- How much time do you spend in the past, in nostalgia, or in the future, on plans?

- Have you ever considered that now is your only reality – here and now?

In the presence of the Holy One

Lord, in your presence
we have nothing to say, nothing to bring,
nothing that will make you love us more,
or convince you of our worth,
nothing to prove.
Nothing.

We will never be able to capture in words
your abundance, your steadfast love, your forgiveness,
but only catch a glimpse, perhaps,
like the kingfisher's wing flashing past us.

Help us to let go –
to unstrap our armour,
let down our defences,
and sit here in the presence
that does not judge,
does not calculate,
does not change.

We can only bring our poverty,
our confession that we are sinners,
our open, wounded hearts,
our silence,

and in the silence make room for you,
let you come alive in us,
hear our name spoken,
and know that we are loved
and called.

But the tax collector, standing far off, would not even look up to heaven, but was beating his breast and saying, "God be merciful to me, a sinner!" I tell you, this man went down to his home justified rather than the other; for all who exalt themselves will be humbled, but all who humble themselves will be exalted.

Luke 18:13-14

The devout Christian of the future will either be a "mystic", one who has experienced "something", or he will cease to be anything at all.

Karl Rahner, "Christians Living Formerly and Today"[54]

Contemplation is not, first and foremost, a technique for prayer. Sometimes prayer, especially centering prayer, can help us find it, but contemplation is something more. It's a way of being present to what's really inside our own experience. We are in solitude, in contemplation, in prayer, when we feel the warmth of a blanket, taste the flavour of coffee, share love and friendship, and perform the everyday tasks of our lives so as to perceive in them that our lives aren't little or anonymous or unimportant, but that what's timeless and eternal is in the ordinary of our lives.

Ronald Rolheiser, Prayer[55]

Let nothing disturb you,
Let nothing frighten you,
All things are passing away:
God never changes.
Patience obtains all things
Whoever has God lacks nothing;
God alone suffices.

St Teresa of Avila

Can I change?

A prayer for Lent

Lord, in this holy season,
give me the grace to change, to believe I can be changed,
to take small steps towards my true self –
from selfishness to service,
from judgment to mercy,
from anxiety to faith.

In this holy season,
help me to give time to prayer
as you did so often: before a major decision,
at the end of a long day of coming and going,
in the time of trial.
Help me to spend time with you every day,
to set aside my relentless thoughts,
and abide in you
in silence and trust.

In this holy season,
help me to fast from what is holding me back
from becoming my true self: my addictions
to the pleasures of the body,
to the mental habits which dull my attention,
to the habits of a lifestyle
which could never be shared with everyone on the planet.
Help me to choose my fasting wisely,
and to persevere, with your grace.

In this holy season,
help me to give alms to my neighbours in need,
and not just my spare change,
but to better understand their needs,
the pain, hidden in plain sight,
to give of my time and imagination
to help those who are vulnerable,
to build the kingdom in my community.

And in this holy season, Lord,
help me not to despair when I fall at the first hurdle,
but to remember your generosity to the labourers
who came along at the end,
as much as to those who were there
from the beginning.

> As a deer longs for flowing streams,
>   so my soul longs for you, O God.
> My soul thirsts for God,
>   for the living God.
> When shall I come and behold
>   the face of God?
>
> Psalm 42:1-2

> The interior penance of the Christian can be expressed in
> many and various ways. Scripture and the Fathers insist above
> all on three forms, fasting, prayer, and almsgiving, which
> express conversion in relation to oneself, to God, and to others.
>
> *Catechism of the Catholic Church*, 1434

Conversion is accomplished in daily life by gestures of reconciliation, concern for the poor, the exercise and defense of justice and right, by the admission of faults to one's brethren, fraternal correction, revision of life, examination of conscience, spiritual direction, acceptance of suffering, endurance of persecution for the sake of righteousness. Taking up one's cross each day and following Jesus is the surest way of penance.

Catechism of the Catholic Church, 1435

When I'm wondering what to do in Lent

Father, this year I thought that, instead of giving up something, I'd write a list for Lent. In these actions may I be better prepared to journey to Easter and to share in the pattern of your Son's death and the glory of his resurrection. In these humble gestures may my love of you and my love of neighbour become entwined and united. This Lent, open my heart to recognize that I'm best placed to serve you when I'm serving others.

This Lent, Father, give me the grace to [amend as appropriate]:

Choose a virtue, stick a note of it on my fridge and
    pray for it each time I see it. ☐

Pray once a week for someone I'm struggling to like. ☐

Admit to sin I have committed and seek your healing. ☐

Take myself less seriously at work. ☐

Stay in a few times and give the money I would have
    spent to those who are poor. ☐

Say "thank you" in prayer for something I take for granted. ☐

Visit a person who lives alone. ☐

Listen generously (properly) to someone, without interrupting. ☐

Reduce the waste I create and the mess I make. ☐

Tell someone about your unconditional love for them. ☐

Father, these are just small steps in the right direction… homeward bound. By your grace give me the courage to start here and to journey onwards, building with your Son the kingdom he spoke of.

Amen.

Whenever you pray, do not be like the hypocrites… whenever you fast, do not look dismal… when you give alms, do not let your left hand know what your right hand is doing.

Matthew 6:5, 16, 3

Personal reflection

- Is it time to rethink Lent and be more imaginative about prayer, fasting and giving to people in need?

◆ Examination of conscience

For group or individual use.

Lord, help me to examine my life with honesty,
knowing that I have nothing to hide from you,
knowing that you are not judging me,
knowing that you know me better than I know myself.

Who have I ignored who is in need of my time at the moment?
Whose dignity do I routinely disregard?
Who have I locked in with unforgiveness?

Who have I hurt with a deliberately chosen word or phrase in
their company, or online?
Who have I diminished with gossip or rumour?
Who have I not stood up for when they were being victimized?

Do I know who's vulnerable in my life, in my neighbourhood?
Do I reach out to them in any way?
Do I give any thought to the origins of what I consume, or wear?

Do I indulge in negative thinking, allowing it to dominate my
mood for long periods?
Do I indulge my fantasies, ignoring the danger that my thoughts
can become my words, then my actions?
Do I indulge my small self, the one who looks for the path of
least resistance?

Do I give any time to prayer?

Do I make any space to listen to the prompting of the Spirit in my conscience?

Do I take any time to lose myself in the wonder of creation?

What do I treasure?

Where is my heart?

Where does it need to be?

Your beliefs become your thoughts,
Your thoughts become your words,
Your words become your actions,
Your actions become your habits,
Your habits become your values,
Your values become your destiny.

Attributed to various people, including
Ralph Waldo Emerson and Mahatma Gandhi

When I catch myself being fake

Creator God, you did not create us adorned in jewels or makeup, protected by armour, united by neatly ironed uniforms, or dressed in liturgical finery. Help me to have the courage to recover the beauty of my naked self, the real me, and stand before you as you made me. Give me the courage for my inner self to grow strong. May I stand in your court with no need to be ashamed. Have mercy on this covered disciple still hiding, who knows one thing: that your mercy is greater.

When I say the wrong things to make the right impression:
Lord, have mercy.
When I come to a place to be seen rather than to see:
Lord, have mercy.
When I'm networking for advantage rather than service:
Lord, have mercy.
When I'm pleasing the crowd and not my conscience:
Lord, have mercy.
When my promises are for effect rather than impact:
Lord, have mercy.
When I do the right things for the wrong reasons:
Lord, have mercy.
When I use authority to assert my significance and not yours:
Lord, have mercy.
When my self-importance consumes my true significance:
Lord, have mercy.
When I allow the mirror to determine my self-worth:
Lord, have mercy.
When I type words I'd never say to someone's face:
Lord, have mercy.

When I compare myself with others and then diminish myself:

Lord, have mercy.

When I keep quiet rather than speak the truth:

Lord, have mercy.

Creator God, help me to be your creation and not a creation of my own making. May I not deny the world who you created me to be. Help me to find the strength to be truly, authentically, honestly and courageously... me! Nothing more. Nothing less.

Amen.

> I pray that, according to the riches of his glory, he may grant that you may be strengthened in your inner being with power through his Spirit, and that Christ may dwell in your hearts through faith.
>
> Ephesians 3:16-17

> Becoming a saint means becoming more fully yourself, becoming what the Lord wished to dream and create, and not a photocopy... If you simply copy someone else, you will deprive this earth, and heaven too, of something that no one else can offer.
>
> Pope Francis, *Christus Vivit*[56]

Personal reflection

- How good are you at being you?

When I regret the things I've done

Lord, there are times when I look back and see with adult eyes the pain I caused in years gone by.

The comment I made to the girl about her coat that her mom had bought on sale. The coat was probably all her mom could afford. My joking made the girl want more than her mom could give. The ridicule was cheap and the pain was expensive.

I think of all the thoughtlessness that comes from my insecurity: jokes that others pay the price for; jokes to win the approval of the crowd.

Lord, undo the knots that we tie in the hearts of others. Send your Spirit upon the trail of damage that our thoughtlessness causes. Heal those we have hurt. May our regret become our teacher.

Lord, please heal the hurt we have caused and help us to do it no more, that we in turn undo the countless knots tied in the hearts of others.

Amen.

> Zacchaeus stood there and said to the Lord, "Look, half of my possessions, Lord, I will give to the poor; and if I have defrauded anyone of anything, I will pay back four times as much."
>
> Luke 19:8

Personal reflection

- Is regret a good thing?

- What does it mean to have a healthy conscience?

About prayer

It's about humility, not merit.

It's about honesty, not best behaviour.

It's about the heart, not the head.

It's about faith, not certainty.

It's about simplicity, not complexity.

It's about friendship, not fear.

It's about intimacy, not distance.

It's about community, not just me.

It's about routine, not whenever.

It's about changing our mind, not God's.

It's about what we undergo, not what we do.

It's about being called into being.

It's about being loved.

And, being loved, loving others, loving the world...

> We really live outside of ourselves. There are very few humans who truly live inside themselves and this is why there are so many problems... In each person's heart, there is something like a small, intimate space, where God comes down to speak alone with that person. And this is where a person determines his or her own destiny, his or her own role in the world.
>
> Oscar Romero, *Through the Year with Oscar Romero*[57]

> Prayer is not asking. Prayer is putting oneself in the hands of God, at his disposition, and listening to his voice in the depth of our hearts.
>
> Mother Teresa

Whom do we serve?

For Holy Thursday

Whom do we serve? Who serves us?
What do we do with our power? What power do we have?
Who do we think we are in this world?
What are we here for? To serve
or to be served?

Lord, you showed us the way.
For the avoidance of doubt, your best sermons
were what you *did*, like at the Last Supper: on your knees,
washing the dusty feet of your disciples.
This was too much for Peter, still not getting it,
despite all that time spent together.

On your last night,
just hours away from the madness
of trial by the human race, you gave us
no less than yourself,
and made it very simple for all those who dared
to follow you: do the same.

> This is where the way that Jesus talks about holiness at the Last
> Supper is so transforming. Holiness there is seen as going into the
> heart of where it's most difficult for human beings to be human.
> Jesus goes "outside the city"; he goes to the place where people
> suffer and are humiliated, the place where people throw stuff out,
> including other people.
>
> Rowan Williams, *Being Disciples*[58]

When I'm reluctant to go on

Enemies schemed.
They ignored your wisdom because of your parentage,
murdered your cousin,
berated you for the company you kept
and made plans to kill you for the teaching you gave.
Yet you carried on loving.

Friends failed.
They competed for your favour,
sought privilege in knowing you,
slept when your hour came,
betrayed you
and were nowhere to be seen in your humiliation.
Yet you carried on loving.

Authorities abused.
They accused you with false evidence,
tried you without integrity,
manipulated crowds to condemn you
and used a brutal army to torture you.
Yet you carried on loving.

Followers argue.
As your followers, we have argued over which songs to sing,
which rules must come first,
which church is the best,
who gets the credit.
Yet you carry on loving us.

Lord, thank you for not giving up on us.

When I think my life is hard, help me to carry on loving. Like you do.

Amen.

> Then Jesus told his disciples, "If any want to become my followers, let them deny themselves and take up their cross and follow me. For those who want to save their life will lose it, and those who lose their life for my sake will find it."
>
> Matthew 16:24-25

Personal reflection

- There is a lot of talk these days about resilience. What sort of resilience is needed to follow Jesus?

What happened on Good Friday?

The Gospels don't go into much detail.
They don't have to.
Most people in the ancient world
knew all about crucifixion,
may well have walked underneath the death rattle
of slaves and rebels
nailed up to die
on the roadside on the way into the city.
The message was simple:
if you threaten the established order,
this will happen to you.

And yet, Lord,
this is where we find you –
a naked, dying victim,
condemned by the world,
defeated by the kingdom of violence,
heaving for breath,
fixed to a high gibbet outside
the city walls:
the revelation of the innermost being of God.

You took upon yourself our violence,
the worst things we do to each other,
absorbed it all in your body –
let it penetrate
to the very heart of God
and then, looking out
over the blurred, leering crowd, somehow
forgave us.

My children,

I know what you're like.

I know what you do. It's not your fault.

Despite everything,

I still want to take you to a new place, a new order, a new kingdom –

with no victims, no scapegoats,

where the lost, the last and the least

are looked after,

where tenderness is the order of the day,

where you walk in peace

with your humble, limping God,

your forgiven neighbour,

and know what

you're doing.

> My God, my God, why have you forsaken me?
> Why are you so far from helping me, from the words of my
> groaning?
>
> Psalm 22:1

As he hung from the cross, he *became* sin, as Saint Paul would later put it, and bearing the full weight of that disorder he said, "Father, forgive them, they know not what they do" (Luke 23:34). Jesus on the cross drowned all the sins of the world in the infinite ocean of the divine mercy, and that is how he fought.

Robert Barron, *Catholicism*[59]

When my father died

I could take you to the very spot.
A café in a highway service station overlooking the traffic
heading madly north and south,
an empty coffee cup on the Formica top in front of me.
My brother phoned me, said that dad was gone, I was too late.
   He was spirit.
And when I got back in the car and headed on north,
less in a hurry now, wiping away tears,
I was glad that, on my last visit, sitting on his hospital bed,
I said to him, for the first time, "I love you, Dad."
By then, he was far removed from who he had been,
but when he heard that, his blue eyes flared
and he tried to sit up.
Our whole life, our difficult years,
coming to a point of grace that afternoon
at the end of visiting hours.

Now he is spirit,
and I am glad that once, just once,
I let go and said the one thing that freed us both
from the knots of pride
and pain.

Lord, this kind of loss is not easy.
When a parent dies,
one who was there for us over the years, through it all,
no matter what the age, or illness beforehand,
it knocks the wind out of us, opens up a great gap in our being.

We cling to those we love, those we know,
so it's hard to let go, to imagine the bigger life they inhabit still.
We cramp with grief, just as you did
when your friend Lazarus died, or when your father Joseph died
unbeknown to history, of a fever, an injury at work, we don't know.
But we imagine you with him in his final hard hours,
the man who taught you the ways of God,
the workings of wood and stone, an honest day's labour.

Dear Lord,
who knew the pain of human loss,
be with all those who mourn, comfort them
in their dark, lonely hours,
may they find some strength from faith and friends
to get through, to sort out the day,
and then, one day, to wake to the morning light
and figure it will all go on,
and they will go on,
with a heart more tender for having loved.

But the souls of the righteous are in the hand of God,
and no torment will ever touch them.
In the eyes of the foolish they seemed to have died,
and their departure was thought to be a disaster,
and their going from us to be their destruction;
but they are at peace.

Wisdom 3:1-3

When health fails the elderly

As I look into the face of this fragile woman
whose body is now bent and skin now weathered;
help me to see the child within her, holding the doll she once
   cherished.
Help me to see the little girl running through fields of barley in a
   lilac dress.
Help me to see her dreaming of love's embrace.
Help me to look beyond the tired eyes and weary bones.
Help me to see her holding her own children to the sky in elevated joy.
Help me to see her crouching to point out the dragonfly or dandelion.
Help me to see the skills she acquired and all those plates she spun.
Help me to remember that she saved carefully,
persevered resiliently,
worked tirelessly
and gave endlessly.

When autumn falls upon those we love, help us to see their
springtime, too. Once upon another time, they, too, had young hopes
and dreams as yet unfulfilled. Let not their shrinking horizons
diminish the lives they once led. Help me to see that each falling leaf
enjoyed a long summer.

Lord, in loving those whose health now fails, grant us patience and
stamina. Whether they loved us as they should have done or fell short
of the mark, grant us the ability to accompany them with tenderness.
In your time, call them forth to meet your Father.

Amen.

During the Synod, one of the young auditors from the Samoan Islands spoke of the Church as a canoe, in which the elderly help to keep on course by judging the position of the stars, while the young keep rowing, imagining what waits for them ahead. Let us steer clear of young people who think that adults represent a meaningless past, and those adults who always think they know how young people should act. Instead, let us all climb aboard the same canoe and together seek a better world, with the constantly renewed momentum of the Holy Spirit.

Pope Francis, *Christus Vivit*[60]

Personal reflection

- Why is it important to look beyond a person's frailty?

In the tomb

Today we pray for all those

in the tomb of abuse
in the tomb of exploitation
in the tomb of poverty

in the tomb of addiction
in the tomb of grief
in the tomb of loneliness

in the tomb of self-image
in the tomb of guilt
in the tomb of depression.

Lord, who knew the very darkest places of the human condition,
who knew the silence of death,
grant that we may see you in our darkness.

Hold out your hand to us
and lead us to the light.

> So Joseph took the body and wrapped it in a clean linen cloth and
> laid it in his own new tomb, which he had hewn in the rock. He
> then rolled a great stone to the door of the tomb and went away.
> Mary Magdalene and the other Mary were there, sitting opposite
> the tomb.
>
> Matthew 27:59-61

What needs to rise in us?

Whatever was dead in the darkness,
laid out behind the hard-to-move boulder
on a ledge in the new tomb, shrouded hastily,
dead all through the long Saturday of shock and silence,
did not rise in their *imagination*,
nor come to life in their hearts after months of remembering
what he said and did.

No.

Something happened
to the dead prophet, Jesus of Nazareth,
to the small, dead body of the executed carpenter-turned-messiah.
The love of the Father detonated
inside the dead man,
flooding every atom with transfigured life.
No one was there to record this event.
If any guards did see it, they didn't think to sell their story
and retire to the coast with a plot of land – and a memory
that would haunt every dawn.

What we do know is that the tomb
was found to be empty by the women in the frail first light.
We do know that the risen Lord appeared to Peter the denier,
to the twelve, to five hundred, to James and then to Paul the persecutor,
and the forgiveness of that presence transformed
the broken and bemused
into witnesses, preachers on a mission, unbothered
by the bombast and beatings of the world.

Help us to know, Lord,
what lies in the tomb of our hearts,
what long-dead life needs to be woken by grace,
what memory needs to stagger out, still bandaged,
and feel the sunlight of forgiveness;
what love lies there, wrapped in the shroud of long indifference?

Easter morning

Here we are in the garden, where it all started.
Where it all went wrong.
A long time after we were shown the way out,
a solitary woman comes back – broken
by the grief of the world.
There is just enough light to make out the shape
of the rock. She remembers the tomb
that the wrapped body
was carried into hastily on the Friday;
the four or five it took to roll the stone into place.
She makes her way, head down, fearful
of attention. She looks up into
a black hole, the stone leaning to the side.

Peter and the Beloved One, summoned in a dream,
filled the early morning with breathless commentary,
 a quick look around
and then running, doing what they do. Men on a mission.
Mary was alone again, in the spreading light, breaking her heart
by the empty tomb. *Where was he?*
More men from somewhere, asking unhelpful questions:
"Why are you weeping?"
And then the gardener, a long time after the last encounter.
So long she didn't recognize him
until the morning sang her name, "Mary!"

Lord, we long to meet you
in the garden, to cling to you like Mary
on the first day of the new creation.
But we must learn what you taught her so gently,
not to cling to the memory of your days among us, your voice
and closeness, by the lake, sitting in the shade.
Your presence now fills more than our vision,
fills the dark world with the light
of tenderness.

Resurrection is the problem

Suffering is not the problem.
Lord, I mean that suffering is straightforward.
I know suffering – not so much in my life,
but what I've seen and heard. It's dreadful, of course,
and please spare those I love from suffering,
spare all who suffer.
But what I mean is it's there and it calls me out
to do something about it, or walk away, talk over it
while it's trying to get my attention.
I think I'm happier in that world – either guilty or angry, my ego
more or less in one piece, negotiating the suffering of the world,
speaking up for justice, brave
from a safe distance.

Lord, my problem is resurrection.
What I struggle with is any real openness
to your risen life, to letting go,
to letting you come alive in me, letting you "take place" in me –
balanced on the high ledge of grace,
with faith in the life you offer, without condition.
That is not straightforward, and it scares me.
I am not good with heights, nor depth for that matter.
Help me to let go, to fall,
knowing you are there.

Emmaus – the long walk home

The disciples on the road to Emmaus
might have been Cleopas
and his wife, who stayed at the foot of the cross to the bitter, bloody end.
So let's imagine we have a married couple on the road of despondency,
arguing with each other about what their hopes had been,
who let who down, and where were you anyway when it mattered?
They have nothing left but their bitterness.
The only energy they can summon
takes them away from the place of hope.
But still they travel together,
holding on, perhaps, to a memory
of what they once had.

Lord, the road of marriage is not easy.
At times it feels like a long, slow walk from a scene of better days.
We "had hoped" for so much
from each other, from our children, from our lives.
And all we hold in the end
is disappointment.
Lord, it's not easy to admit
that the problem may have been ours in the first place.
We had the wrong dreams – we thought the other would answer all
    our needs,
the passion would burn forever;
we thought the children would always need us and want to be with us.
We were reading the wrong script.
We need you by our side to open up the book of life
and help us to see each other,
to recognize the beauty we live with

in the touch of a hand, in the breaking of bread,
in the moment when we, somehow, find it in us
to let go of the hurt we protect like a secret treasure
and take part in resurrection,
not the stone-splitting, earth-moving resurrections of CinemaScope,
but the little resurrections
of the heart.

Some natural tears they dropp'd, but wiped them soon;
The world was all before them, where to choose
Their place of rest, and Providence their guide:
They, hand in hand, with wandering steps and slow,
Through Eden took their solitary way.

John Milton, *Paradise Lost*[61]

It is not your love that sustains the marriage,
but from now on, the marriage that sustains your love.

Dietrich Bonhoeffer, *Letters and Papers from Prison*[62]

As the reality of God has faded from so many lives in the West,
there has been a corresponding inflation of expectations that
personal relations alone will supply meaning and happiness in
life. This is to load our partner with too great a burden. We are
all incomplete: we all need the love which is secure, rather than
oppressive, we need mutual forgiveness, to thrive.

Bishop of London's sermon at the wedding of
Prince William and Kate Middleton, April 29, 2011[63]

When religion is boring[64]

He isn't asking you to give up going to parties.

He isn't asking you to please people.

He isn't asking you to be ashamed.

He isn't asking you to be Pope Francis or Mother Teresa.

He isn't asking you to pretend to be religious.

He isn't asking you to be faultless.

He isn't asking you to live without doubts.

He isn't asking you to be successful.

He isn't asking you to obey things without asking "why?"

He isn't asking you to give up all the things you love to do.

He isn't asking you to avoid risk.

He isn't asking you to think that your sexuality is dirty.

He isn't asking you to meet other people's expectations.

He isn't asking you to make everyone proud of you.

He isn't asking you to like people you secretly dislike.

He isn't asking you to pretend you don't get bored at church things.

He isn't asking you to accept abuse.

He isn't asking you to accept your limitations as if you can't change.

He just isn't. He never did!

So what is he asking?

He asks us to be joyful, knowing we lose our perspective.

He asks us to love... not just the people we like.

He asks us to pray, knowing that we can't live by our
own strength alone.

He asks us to forgive people, because revenge eats away
from the inside.

He asks us not to be afraid of people we don't understand.

He asks us to have the courage not to feel threatened.

He asks us to greet warmly the person in need.

He asks us to smell advantage dressed as service and to dare to challenge it.

He asks us to pray for wisdom, knowing which fights to pick and when.

He asks us to have courage to challenge people like me, who sit here and write things.

So it is not all coffee and cake... sometimes it costs us dearly.

But there is no life worth living more than *being his!*

When Jesus turned and saw them following, he said to them, "What are you looking for?" They said to him, "Rabbi... where are you staying?" He said to them, "Come and see."

John 1:38-39

Personal reflection

- Jesus is the way, the truth and the life. Sometimes we can get the wrong impression of what he wants. What does Jesus ask of you?

When God's Spirit is hidden in plain sight

Spirit of the living God, everyone knows it when you touch their lives but no one seems able to describe you. You are a dove hovering; you are a tongue of fire descending; you are the breath of life in our lungs; you are a wind of turmoil disturbing; you are wellsprings of living water; you are wine for our joy; you are a paraclete, an advocate; you are the third person of the Blessed Trinity; you are almighty power bringing life to a seamless void – but who are you to me?

When my days are done and my hour has finally come, this then, Spirit of the living God, is my hope for the ordinary days. That I will meet you in the heavenly realm and declare: "It was you! Look, everyone... it was you!" To my amazement you were there all the time. You were always there.

You were just behind Alison when I met her and you were laughing because you knew she was the one I'd marry. You were up all night with us on the landing when the children were sick. You were standing next to the door at my dad's funeral with a handkerchief, weeping.

You were the one in the empty chair at the interview, shouting, "This isn't for you... there is a better way!" I pray that in the heavenly realm I'll declare, "It was you!" You in the corridor that day saying, "Listen to this man; I have chosen him to speak my words. Be open to what he is going to say." It was you nudging me to help the man in the post office who had just found out that his wife had cancer.

Spirit of the living God, may I discover you were there all the time. Laughing, crying, prompting, enjoying each day with us, not only in the spectacular tongues of fire, but also in the exam hall, the hospital, the nightclub and at the bus stop.

And I hope to discover that you were laughing at all my silly ways and my useless worry, and engineering countless moments of irony, sewing together that tapestry that turned out to be... my life.

Spirit of the living God, fall afresh on me. Every day. Whether I recognize you or not.

Amen.

> And I will ask the Father, and he will give you another Advocate, to be with you forever.
>
> John 14:16

Personal reflection

• How do we sense God's presence or absence in our lives?

Everyone is welcome

You are welcome if you like deep dish pizza or count the calories.

You are welcome if you prefer the main street stores or shop online.

You are welcome if you got drunk last night or haven't touched a drop in forty years.

You are welcome if you passed with distinction, barely passed, or failed it.

You are welcome if you have an impressive career, a tedious career or no career.

You are welcome if you got 14,000 likes or if you think "Outlook" is a weather forecast.

You are welcome if you want friendly fellowship or dignified solitude.

You are welcome if you go to church daily, at Christmas or to avoid the rain.

You are welcome if you voted in, out, right, left, up, down or can never decide.

You are welcome if your body is black, white, brown, wrinkled, worn out, faulty, enhanced, stretched, freckled, toned, tattooed, pierced, or less than a few months old.

You are welcome if you have just fallen in love or are crippled by separation.

You are welcome if you are torn between choices or have no choices to make.

You are welcome if your kids turned out well or cause you worry.

You are welcome if you think yourself useless or gifted.

You are welcome if you are elated or depressed by the results of the pregnancy test.

You are welcome if you are straight, gay, bisexual, transgender, confused, upside down, inside out, or scared of working it out...

Jesus loved, welcomed and forgave. May we never be so polished a community that the untidy are reluctant to come in. May we never expect everyone else to look, sound and behave just as we do in order to be part of us. Should everyone in our community begin to look and sound a bit like us, may we have the courage to do something about it.

Amen.

It is confined to no place or nation, teaches everything needed for salvation, welcomes people of every class, rulers and subjects, learned and ignorant, forgives every kind of sin, and mediates the grace for every kind of virtue.

St Cyril of Jerusalem

Personal reflection

- What circles do we draw around who is welcome and who isn't?

Evening Mass – the people were shining

On Pentecost Sunday
I may have had a slight hangover,
so I went to evening Mass, the "quiet" Mass,
the one with the feeling of an aftermath,
as if you've missed the main event.
We heard in the readings about the Spirit that sounded like a
    mighty wind
and sent the disciples into the street, sparkling
with divine intoxication.
We heard this with our usual attention: some reading the bulletin,
some trying to contain restless children, some nodding off.
The Great Amen sounded more like "Are we there yet?"
but at least the final "Thanks be to God"
was heartfelt.

Afterwards we filed out
into the early evening, a golden light
warming the sandstone of the houses, the parked cars, the trees.
Most were in a hurry to get going, a few
stopped to chat, children running rings around them,
the oldest old waiting to be led,
and I thought just then
of Thomas Merton and his epiphany
on the corner of Fourth and Walnut in Louisville,
when he felt a great oneness with people.
He saw the secret beauty of their hearts,
but there was no way of telling them they were all walking around
shining like the sun.

Spirit of God,
shake my mediocrity, my normality,
my stubborn refusal to be transformed, to be filled
with a power that would ask me
to be new, to be myself,
my deep self, to see others as gift, sheer gift –
forgiven, loved, lit from within,
and to take that Good News
to the ends of the earth.

> Then he opened their minds to understand the scriptures, and he
> said to them, "Thus it is written, that the Messiah is to suffer and
> to rise from the dead on the third day, and that repentance and
> forgiveness of sins is to be proclaimed in his name to all nations,
> beginning from Jerusalem. You are witnesses of these things."
>
> Luke 24:45-48

Endnotes and references

1   Pope Francis, *Evangelii Gaudium* ("The Joy of the Gospel"), 164.

2   @Pontifex, 28 June 2014.

3   Ronald Rolheiser, *Prayer: Our Deepest Longing* (Cincinnati: Franciscan Media, 2013), viii.

4   John O'Donohue, *Benedictus: A Book of Blessings* (London: Bantam Press, 2007), 27.

5   Enzo Bianchi, *Why Pray, How to Pray* (London: St Paul's, 2014), 49.

6   Stephen Bullivant, *The Trinity: How Not to Be a Heretic* (New York: Paulist Press, 2015), 4, 16.

7   Ronald Rolheiser, *Prayer: Our Deepest Longing* (Cincinnati: Franciscan Media, 2013), vii.

8   Pope Francis, *Evangelii Gaudium*, 88.

9   Inspired by the teaching of St. Francis de Sales and by a station announcement.

10   Pope Benedict XVI, *Deus Caritas Est* ("God is Love"), 31.

11   Saints commended by Pope Francis for being known for a sense of humour. *Gaudete et Exsultate* ("On the Call to Holiness in Today's World"), 126.

12   St. John Paul II, *Novo Millennio Ineunte* ("At the Beginning of the New Millennium"), 43.

13   www.rcsouthwark.co.uk/romero_prayer.html, accessed October 21, 2019.

14   Karl Rahner, "Secular Life and the Sacraments: A Copernican Revolution," *The Tablet* (March 6 and 13, 1971).

15   This prayer is based on the Examen, a method of prayer developed by St. Ignatius of Loyola, who founded the Society of Jesus, or the Jesuits. More information on the Examen and other Ignatian techniques can be found at: www.ignatianspirituality.com/ignatian-prayer/the-examen, accessed January 2, 2020.

16   George Herbert, "Prayer." www.poetryfoundation.org/poems/44371/prayer-i, accessed January 14, 2020.

17   Pope Francis, *Christus Vivit* ("Christ is Alive"), 20.

18   "Proclamation Appointing a National Fast Day," March 30, 1863. www.abrahamlincolnonline.org/lincoln/speeches/fast.htm, accessed March 4, 2020.

19   Walter Brueggemann, *Sabbath as Resistance: Saying No to the Culture of Now* (Louisville: Westminster John Knox Press, 2014), 85.

20   Pope Francis, *Gaudete et Exsultate*, 108.

21   Robert Barron, *Catholicism: A Journey to the Heart of the Faith* (New York: Image Books, 2011), 91.

22   Thomas Merton, *Raids on the Unspeakable* (New York: New Directions, 1964), 72.

23   Pope Francis, *Gaudete et Exsultate*, 101.

24   Ronald Rolheiser, "The Christ-Child of the Year." http://ronrolheiser. com/the-christ-child-of-the-year, accessed December 30, 2019.

25   Inspired by Pope Francis, *Amoris Laetitia* ("The Joy of Love"), chapter 5 – "Love Made Fruitful."

26   Pope Francis, *Amoris Laetitia*, 166.

27   Pope Francis, *Evangelii Gaudium*, 3.

28   Thomas Keating, *Invitation to Love: The Way of Christian Contemplation* (London: Continuum, 2012), 11.

29   Joan Chittister, *In God's Holy Light: Wisdom from the Desert Monastics* (Cincinnati: Franciscan Media, 2015), 42.

30   Pope Francis in Chile, January 16, 2018. http://w2.vatican.va/ content/francesco/en/speeches/2018/january/documents/ papa-francesco_20180116_cile-santiago-religiosi.html, accessed March 4, 2020.

31   Emily Dickinson, "If I Can Stop One Heart from Breaking." www.poemhunter.com/poem/if-i-can-stop-one-heart-from-breaking, accessed March 1, 2020.

32   Henri Nouwen, *In the Name of Jesus: Reflections on Christian Leadership* (New York: Darton, Longman and Todd, 1989), 16.

33 Rowan Williams, *Being Disciples: Essentials of Christian Life* (London: SPCK, 2016), 11.

34 C. S. Lewis, *The Weight of Glory: A Collection of Lewis' Most Moving Addresses* (London: William Collins, 2013), 45.

35 Second Vatican Council, *Gaudium et Spes* (Pastoral Constitution on the Church in the Modern World), 3.

36 Pope Francis, *Laudato Si'* ("On Care for Our Common Home"), 65.

37 Ronald Rolheiser, *Prayer*, 22.

38 Pope Francis, *Gaudete et Exsultate*, 52.

39 Inspired by the passion narratives and Matt Redman & Jonas Myrin, *10,000 Reasons (Bless the Lord)* (Kingsway Music, 2011). www.youtube.com/watch?v=XtwIT8JjddM, accessed 28 October 2019.

40 Elizabeth Barrett Browning, "Aurora Leigh," in D. H. S. Nicholson & A. H. E. Lee, *The Oxford Book of English Mystical Verse* (Oxford: OUP, 1917), 86.

41 Thomas Merton, *New Seeds of Contemplation* (New York: New Directions, 1961), 30.

42 Pope Francis, *Laudato Si'*, 50.

43 Inspired by the hymn "How Great Thou Art," by Stuart K. Hine; "Lord for Tomorrow" by Sister M. Xavier; and *Laudato Si'*.

44 Pope Francis, *Laudato Si'*, 80.

45 Gerard Manley Hopkins, "Pied Beauty." www.poetryfoundation.org/poems/44399/pied-beauty, accessed 28 October 2019.

46 Walter Brueggemann, *Sabbath as Resistance*, 18.

47 Dietrich Bonhoeffer, *Prayers from Prison: Prayers and Poems* (Philadelphia: Fortress Press, 1978), 27.

48 Thomas Merton, *Love and Living* (New York: Farrar, Straus & Giroux, 1979), 11.

49 Thomas Keating, *Open Mind, Open Heart: The Contemplative Dimension of the Gospel* (London: Continuum, 2006), 59.

50   John Donne, "Batter My Heart", https://www.poetryfoundation.org/poems/44106/holy-sonnets-batter-my-heart-three-person-god, accessed March 8, 2020.

51   Dorothee Soelle, *Death by Bread Alone: Texts and Reflections on Religious Experience* (Philadelphia: Fortress Press, 1978), 6.

52   Eckhart Tolle, *The Power of Now: A Guide to Spiritual Enlightenment* (London: Hodder & Stoughton, 1999), 41.

53   *YOUCAT: Youth Catechism of the Catholic Church* (San Francisco: Ignatius Press, 2011), 282.

54   Karl Rahner, "Christians Living Formerly and Today," in *Theological Investigations, vii*, trans. David Bourke (New York: Herder & Herder, 1971).

55   Ronald Rolheiser, *Prayer*. For more information on the practice of Christian meditation known as "centering prayer," please visit www.contemplativeoutreach.org/category/category/centering-prayer, or read the works of Fr. Thomas Keating, especially *Open Mind, Open Heart*.

56   Pope Francis, *Christus Vivit*, 162.

57   Oscar Romero, *Through the Year with Oscar Romero: Daily Meditations* (London: Darton, Longman & Todd, 2006).

58   Rowan Williams, *Being Disciples*, 48.

59   Robert Barron, *Catholicism: A Journey to the Heart of the Faith* (New York: Image, 2011), 91.

60   Pope Francis, *Christus Vivit*, 201.

61   John Milton, *Paradise Lost*. http://www.gutenberg.org/cache/epub/26/pg26.html, accessed March 4, 2020.

62   Dietrich Bonhoeffer, *Letters and Papers from Prison*. https://quotecatalog.com/quote/dietrich-bonhoeffer-it-is-not-your-zpWoGPp, accessed April 19, 2019.

63   Bishop of London's sermon at the wedding of Prince William and Kate Middleton, April 29, 2011. www.london.anglican.org/articles/royal-wedding, accessed January 3, 2020.

64   Based upon *Gaudete et Exsultate*.

About the authors

Raymond Friel was born in Scotland and, after graduating from Glasgow University, has spent most of his professional life in England. He started teaching in London in 1990 and was a head teacher in Catholic secondary schools from 2002 until 2016. In that time, he was a National Leader of Education and supported other schools in addition to his own. He is currently CEO of Plymouth CAST, a multi-academy trust of thirty-six Catholic schools in the southwest of England. He is the author of a number of influential books on Catholic education and spirituality, including *How to Survive in Leadership in a Catholic School, Gospel Values for Catholic Schools* and *Prayers for Schools*. He is married to Janet, an artist, and they live in Somerset. They have three sons, who have more or less left home.
You can follow Raymond on Twitter: @friel_raymond

David Wells is an international speaker and bestselling author of *The Reluctant Disciple* and *The Grateful Disciple*. He was educated at English Martyrs School in Leicester, at Keele University and later in Liverpool, where he trained as a teacher. In 1994 he was awarded a Master of Philosophy degree from Nottingham University. He began his career as a teacher in Ilkeston, Derbyshire, and went on to work for the Catholic Education Service in London before becoming an adult education advisor. He worked in the Diocese of Nottingham and then in the Diocese of Plymouth. He is a guest lecturer at three universities and two seminaries. As a public speaker David has led and taught all sorts of groups, from speaking to thousands in arenas in the USA or at Wembley Stadium, or to just a few volunteers in a quiet village parish. David is married to Alison. They met in a supermarket when they were young students. She works as an advisory teacher of deaf and hearing-impaired people. Their three children, Sam, Matt and Emily, are fast starting adventures of their own.
David can be reached via his website: davidwellslive.com